DATE DUE FOR RETURN

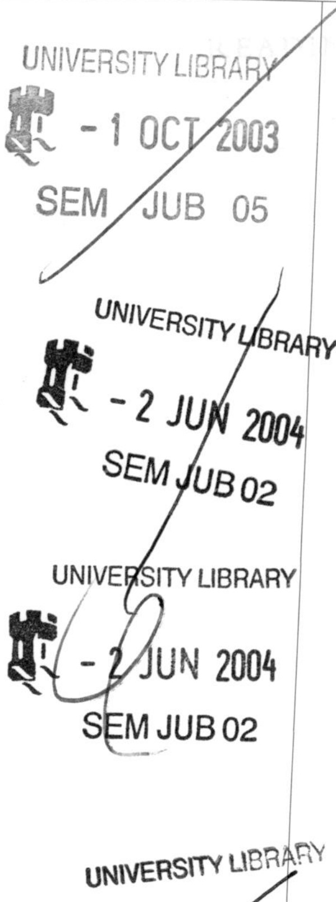

This book may be recalled before the above date.

BY THE SAME AUTHOR

Breaktime
Dance on My Grave
Now I Know
The Toll Bridge
Postcards from No Man's Land
(*recipient 1999 Carnegie Medal*)
Seal Secret
The Present Takers
(*all Bodley Head*)

The Reading Environment
Tell Me: Children, Reading & Talk
Booktalk: Occasional Writing
on Literature and Children
(*all Thimble Press*)

Only Once: A Play
(*Line by Line*)

AIDAN CHAMBERS

Reading Talk

Thimble Press

To MARGARET CLARK

1003131870

ISBN 0 903355 50 7

Copyright © 2001 Aidan Chambers

First published 2001 by The Thimble Press
Lockwood, Station Road, Woodchester
Stroud, Glos. GL5 5EQ
phone 014 5375 5566 fax 014 5387 8599

Printed in Great Britain
by Short Run Press, Exeter

CONTENTS

ABOUT THE COLLECTION

Anne Frank's Pen. Some of the material in this previously unpublished piece has been included in talks and lectures given over recent years. One of the first of these, 'A Question of Value', was presented at the conference of the School Library Association, 15 September 1996; one of the most recent was given during a lecture tour of Sweden in March 2001.

All of a Tremble to See His Danger is the 1986 May Hill Arbuthnot Honor Lecture, sponsored by Scott, Foresman Company and Margaret K McElderry Books in co-operation with the Association for Library Service to Children. It was presented 15 April 1986 and reprinted in the September 1986 issue of *Signal* by permission of the American Library Association.

Schools in Stories: Talbot Baines Reed is the sixth Helen Stubbs Memorial Lecture, given at the Osborne Collection of Early Children's Books, Toronto Public Library, 18 November 1993. It was issued in 1994 by the Library as a separate publication for Friends of the Osborne Collection.

Pick up a Penguin appeared in the January 1993 *Signal*, which was guest-edited by Margaret Clark.

In Spite of Being a Translation was first published in *The Written World: Youth and Literature*, edited by Agnes Nieuwenhuizen, D.W. Thorpe (Australia), 1994.

Something Zeppelin! was given in celebration of Tormod Haugen's fiftieth birthday at a seminar, 3 March - 1 April 1995 at Høgskolen i Hedmark, Norway, and published in *Tormod Haugen—en artikkelsamling*, Gyldendal Norsk, Oslo, 1995, edited by Ola Losløkk and Bjarne Øygarden.

The Future of the Book. An early version of parts of this previously unpublished essay appeared in the 1992 Sidney Robbins Memorial Lecture, 'The Difference of Literature: Writing Now for the Future of Young Readers', published in *Children's Literature in Education*, number 88, 1993.

Anne Frank's Pen

Like all great books *The Diary of Anne Frank* creates its own world. Though rooted in the everyday, it seems to possess a character, a personality, a consciousness, that is peculiar to it.

Like many great books *The Diary of Anne Frank* has generated several industries. Films, theatre and tv dramas are based on it. Various items of merchandise, knick-knacks, postcards, T-shirts, multimedia documentaries, and numerous other books exploit it. It is the subject of classroom study and academic research. People visit the place where its author lived, where the book was written, and where its story is located. It has been translated into many languages. There is endless talk about it. And like all great books, it seems to yield something new every time you reread it. It grows as you grow, changes as you change. Indeed, some of its readers would claim that it is a cause of their growth and change.

The Diary is a great book about what it is like to be an adolescent by someone who was still an adolescent while writing it. This makes it a benchmark, a model, a standard against which to compare and assay youth literature. As well, it raises important issues about the nature of writing as against authoring, about the relationship of the reader and reading to the writer and the written, and the problems and ethics of translation. Above all, it is quite simply a perpetually fascinating work of literature, which itself calls in question what a work we call 'literature' is.

The Diary of Anne Frank was first published in English in 1952, translated by B. M. Mooyaart-Doubleday. This was how it was known until a new translation was published in 1995, *The Diary of a Young Girl: The Definitive Edition* by Anne Frank, translated by Susan Massotty. Between these came *The Diary of Anne Frank: The Critical Edition* prepared by the Netherlands State Institute for War Documentation, published in 1989, the result of the Dutch government's multidisciplinary scientific investigation into the diary, its history, production, materials, and handwriting, conducted in order to prove (which it did) or disprove the authenticity of the book. The English edition used the Mooyaart-Doubleday translation with hitherto unpublished passages—about thirty percent of the original diary—translated by Arnold J. Pomerans.

Here is a paragraph from the first translation:

> I have one outstanding trait in my character, which must strike anyone who knows me for any length of time, and that is my knowledge of myself. I can watch myself and my actions, just like an outsider. The Anne of every day I can face entirely without prejudice, without making excuses for her, and watch what's good and what's bad about her. This "self-consciousness" haunts me, and every time I open my mouth I know as soon as I've spoken whether "that ought to have been different" or "that was right as it was." There are so many things about myself that I condemn; I couldn't begin to name them all. I understand more and more how true Daddy's words were when he said: "All children must look after their own upbringing." Parents can only give good advice or put them on the right paths, but the final forming of a person's character lies in his own hands.

This was written on Saturday 15 July 1944, part of one of the longest and most moving entries of all. Anne was born on 12 June 1929, so she was just fifteen years and one month old when she penned those words. By then she had been in hiding for two years, locked up with five middle-aged adults and two other teenagers in the few barricaded, blacked-out, overcrowded rooms, stuffy in summer, cold in winter, at the back of her father's offices at Prinsengracht 263 in Amsterdam, never once being allowed out since a few days after her thirteenth birthday, when she started writing what we think of as her diary.

Fifteen. I wonder how many fifteen-year-olds could write such a passage? I wonder if you, dear reader, whatever your age, think you could? This I know: I couldn't have written it at fifteen, nor at sixty-five. Let's acknowledge straightaway that we are dealing with an exceptional person.

We need to remember something else. Anne did not write the passage I've quoted, for she did not write in English. She wrote in Dutch. What we are reading is a translation. We also need to keep in mind that Anne's first language was German. She and her family were taken to what was thought to be the safe haven of the neutral Netherlands in February 1934 to avoid a Nazi pogrom. There she joined the infant class at the Montessori school in Amsterdam and started to learn Dutch. So her diary is written in her second language. When I asked my Dutch friends what Anne's Dutch is like, they said it is very accomplished, and—for the time of writing, when grammatical correctness and formal style were required—an unusual and interesting mix of the high and literary with the popular and colloquial. Maybe that's a result of writing in her second language. But isn't it what bookish and literary-minded young people often do, mix the conventionally approved and disapproved colloquial, when they set out rather self-consciously to 'write'? Anne was exceptional in her ability but she was also a typical adolescent in many of her impulses and much of her behaviour: that's obvious from the anecdotes she tells about herself in the diary and is confirmed by Miep Gies, the courageous woman who supported Anne and the others at peril of her own life by bringing them food and books and medicine and news and everything else they needed while in hiding. Her book, *Anne Frank Remembered*, is the best account we have of what Anne was like, written by someone who knew her from soon after the family arrived in Amsterdam and saw her almost every day till the moment she was taken off to the Nazi camps.

Anne had one ambition. She wanted to be a famous author.

While he was still a student at the University of Amsterdam in the 1980s, a Dutch friend of mine, Wilfred Takken, now himself a fine professional writer, told me a story he knew would interest me. He was on his way to the university library one day when he came across two young backpackers, beautiful girls of about his own age, who were talking with American accents. Wilfred was studying American literature and politics so he started a conversation with them. At one point, he mentioned the war. 'Which war?' the Americans asked. 'The Second World War,' Wilfred said. 'Oh,' said the girls, 'were the Dutch in that war?' 'Of course,' Wilfred said. 'We were occupied for five years.' 'Really!' said the girls. 'We didn't know.'

The next day Wilfred was passing the Anne Frank house on Prinsengracht. It was coming up to ten o'clock, and as usual at that time on most days of the year there was a long queue of people waiting to go in. And who should he see in the queue but the two backpackers. 'Hello,' he said. 'What are you doing here?' 'Waiting to go into Anne Frank's house,' the girls said. 'But I thought you didn't know about the Dutch and the war,' Wilfred said. 'You must know about it if you've read Anne Frank's diary.' 'But we haven't read it,' the girls said. 'Then why do you want to see her house?' Wilfred asked. 'Well,' the girls said, 'we know she's a famous writer so we want to see where she lived.'

When I heard the story, I hummed and hawed. Wilfred let me tut-tut in my old man's fashion—Americans! young people today! what's the world coming to!—before he said, 'You're wrong. Anne didn't want to be shut up in those awful rooms for two years. She didn't want to be dragged away to the death camps. All she wanted was to be a famous writer. Well, now she's so famous all over the world that people who know almost nothing about her queue up just to see where she wrote the book they haven't read. I think Anne would be over the moon. She's achieved her ambition. Which of us will ever be as successful?' And of course he was right.

We're told that *The Diary* is one of the most read and translated books in the world. When I ask adults about their reading of it, many of them say that they read it in their teens, and that if they have looked at it since, they've read some bits and not others, and not all of it all through in one go. In fact, what most people remember is not anything in *The Diary* itself but what amounts to a rather garbled, certainly very sketchy version of the story of Anne and the writing of her book. What they know is a legend, a factoid—a few facts but mostly skewed truth, which is not even good as fiction.

If you haven't read *The Diary of Anne Frank* for a long time, let me invite you to give it another go. And this time, read it like a novel, from start to finish and all of it, in as concentrated a time as you can manage. Let me explain why.

*

Among Anne's presents for her thirteenth birthday on Friday 12 June 1942 was a squarish blank-paged book with a red-and-white checked linen cover, intended as an autograph album. It was not a surprise, however, for Anne had chosen it herself when her father bought it for her. That day all she wrote was a kind of prayer: 'I hope I will be able to confide everything to you, as I have never been able to confide in anyone, and I hope you will be a great source of comfort and support'. By Monday 28 September, two-and-a-half months after she and her family went into hiding, she knew just how terribly her hope had come true. That day she appended a PS to the diary's first entry: 'Oh, I'm so glad I brought you along!'

She wrote the second entry on the Sunday two days after her birthday, the third the next day. In them she addresses the diary itself: she talks to it. She writes nothing more till the following Saturday because, she says, she wanted to think about her diary and what to write in it, for who 'will be interested in the musings of a thirteen-year-old schoolgirl?' During this third entry, a long account of herself and her family, she explains: 'I feel like writing, and I have an even greater need to get all kinds of things off my chest'. Later, she adds: 'I want the diary to be my friend, and I'm going to call this friend *Kitty*'. After that, every entry begins *Lieve Kitty*—Dear Kitty—except for a few which begin *Liefste*—Dearest—*Kitty*.

Specialists in the study of diaries remark that beginning diarists, especially girls, often choose someone to address, and the addressee is sometimes invented. It isn't difficult to understand why. Until you know who you're talking to, it's hard to decide what to write about your daily life. I have a friend, for example, who isn't much interested in what I'm reading but does like to hear about what I'm writing. There are friends with whom I discuss my finances and others with whom I wouldn't. It's like this for all of us. Knowing who your reader is dictates—or helps you choose—the subject matter. It also dictates—helps you select—the kind of language you use. I write differently by email to an intimate friend than by snail mail to an unknown business correspondent.

In this mode of communication all writers are reader-dependent.

What some experienced writers know is that there is a shift to be made in this dependent relationship. Years ago Roland Barthes gave us the terms 'readerly' text and 'writerly' text. My own way of expressing it is to talk about writers and authors. Writers write for a known readership. They know what their readers want, the language they prefer, the length, the complexity, the tone. They supply a demand, just as all craft workers must. They expect to make a living from what they produce. They are reader-focused. Authors, on the other hand, are text-focused. Their aim is to produce an object—a poem, a novel, a play, whatever—without, at the time of writing, any consideration of a particular readership. It is not their intention to make a living from their work, and they count themselves lucky if they do. Just as readerly writers submit themselves to the demands of the reader so writerly authors submit themselves to the demands of the writing, the demands the text creates as the work progresses. They often begin with only a vague and intuitive conception of the final text. Instead of working towards a previously known end, they have only a sense of an end and work towards it by discovery. Content, language, length, tone, everything is formed by the needs of the text. When the text is published, it acquires its own readership, a readership so unpredictable it is not easy for publicists and marketing managers to identify and 'target'.

As I read Anne's diary from beginning to end in one go I see this transition, this shift from writer to author, taking place. I see her learning on the job, teaching herself how to become the author she wants to be, even before she is conscious of the difference. I know of no other book that is itself so poignantly the embodiment of this metamorphosis. It happens before one's eyes like a butterfly emerging from the carapace of its chrysalis.

She begins by addressing the little square book in which she is writing. But very soon this proves unsatisfying. Paper doesn't read. It's a cool, blank and unresponsive surface. So Anne does what comes naturally. She chooses someone to write to. She creates Kitty, who only exists as Anne's reader. By nature Anne is a narrative writer, a fictionalist. Everything we know about her proves this. The diary itself is laced with episodes that amount to short stories constructed from the unpromising material of her everyday life confined in those few rooms of the secret annexe. And besides the diary she also wrote many separate pieces deliberately intended as short stories.

I want to look closely at one of the stories included in the diary, but before doing so it's important to notice a small but deeply significant detail in Anne's invention of Kitty. In the entry of Saturday 20 June 1942, where she invents Kitty, she says the reason for starting a diary is that she has no 'real friend' with whom she can be intimately close and with whom she can, as the first translation puts it, 'bring myself to talk of anything outside the common round'. It is then that she adds: 'I want the diary to be my friend, and I'm going to call this friend *Kitty*'. In other words, she is not naming another, imaginary person to address but is naming the diary. In doing this she is attributing to the diary—to her own writing—a person-like consciousness. This is not a consciousness of which she is aware, the consciousness of her own everyday self; rather, she has arranged to address an unknown consciousness, another self, a self she calls Kitty.

Young beginning diarists often invent a reader to address, but they do not usually invest the personality, the consciousness of that reader in the object itself. This is an exceptional move on Anne's part. Surely it indicates a quite different yearning, a different purpose, from the usual? Already, right at the start, the unborn author is seeded in the womb of the young pubescent writer. Not yet aware of what she truly is, she yearns to become it.

The story that best demonstrates Anne's nature as a fictionalist, and also shows her making the shift from writer to author, is the entry for Thursday 11 November 1943, when she was fourteen years and five months old.

One of Anne's most treasured possessions was a fountain pen. A gift from her maternal grandmother for her ninth birthday, it had arrived from Germany in a packet marked with a customs declaration: 'of no commercial value'. As Anne used this pen to write much of her diary from the beginning up to this point in November 1943—not far short of half the book—that labelling is delightfully ironic. This pen of no commercial value helped write one of the most lucrative bestsellers in history. She did not use it to write the 11 November entry or any of the rest of the diary because on Friday 5 November 1943 the pen was lost. But she didn't record this disaster until six days later, when she described the event, not in the usual diary fashion, but as a carefully composed story to which she gave a title, 'Ode to My Fountain Pen. In Memoriam'. Here in the new translation by Susan Massotty is the story after Anne has related the history of the pen:

It was just after five on Friday afternoon. I came out of my room and was about to sit down at the table to write when I was roughly pushed to one side to make room for Margot and Father, who wanted to practise their Latin. The fountain pen remained unused on the table, while its owner, sighing, was forced to make do with a very tiny corner of the table, where she began rubbing beans. That's how we remove mould from the beans and restore them to their original state. At a quarter to six I swept the floor, dumped the dirt into a newspaper, along with the rotten beans, and tossed it into the stove. A giant flame shot up, and I thought it was wonderful that the stove, which had been gasping its last breath, had made such a miraculous recovery.

All was quiet again. The Latin students had left, and I sat down at the table to pick up where I'd left off. But no matter where I looked, my fountain pen was nowhere in sight. I took another look. Margot looked, Mother looked, Father looked, Dussel looked. But it had vanished.

"Maybe it fell in the stove, along with the beans!" Margot suggested.

"No, it couldn't have!" I replied.

But that evening, when my fountain pen still hadn't turned up, we all assumed it had been burned, especially because celluloid is highly inflammable. Our darkest fears were confirmed the next day when Father went to empty the stove and discovered the clip, used to fasten it to a pocket, among the ashes. Not a trace of the gold nib was left. "It must have melted into stone," Father conjectured.

I'm left with one consolation, small though it may be: my fountain pen was cremated, just as I would like to be some day.

Yours, Anne.

Can anyone doubt that this is a fabulous fabulator at work? Of course, the incident really happened, but the treatment of it, the shaping of the episode, the skilled pacing, the economical and pointed use of dialogue (much more must have been said than we're told), the rhythmic repetition—'Margot looked, Mother looked, Father looked, Dussel looked'—which ritualizes, heightens and stylizes the small domestic drama, the distancing of the writer-as-subject to the writer-as-observer by a self-mocking, ironizing move at one point into the third person—'while its owner, sighing'—and the delicate touches of deprecatory humour—the Latin students, the 'miraculous' recovery of the fire that had been gasping its last breath—all, surely, are signs not of a reporter, a journalist, but of a born writer of literary fiction. Proust, greatest of memorial fabulators, transforms incidents from his own life in the same way. What Anne is up to is very obvious in this passage, which she deliberately highlights by giving it a title. But she increasingly does the same thing, though less obviously, in the more ordinary entries as the diary progresses from the beginning to this point, and then with conscious skill and purpose from this point until the end.

Now for another, even more significant event in her life. On Thursday 6 January 1944, two months and ten entries after the ode to her fountain pen, Anne wrote about menstruating. This is the first time she mentions her periods, and records that she has only had three so far.

> I think that what's happening to me is so wonderful, and I don't just mean the changes taking place on the outside of my body, but also those on the inside. I never discuss myself or any of these things with others, which is why I have to talk about them to myself. Whenever I have my period (and that's been only three times), I have the feeling that in spite of all the pain, discomfort and mess, I'm carrying around a sweet secret. So even though it's a nuisance, in a certain way I'm always looking forward to the time when I'll feel that secret inside me once again.

The key words are : 'I have to talk about them to myself.' Anne has discovered what all authors know, that the writing that matters to them is the kind where the author tells herself what she needs to know, something she can communicate to herself in no other way. Anne the writer has become Anne the author, and the author has become her own reader. Author-writers write privately, writer-writers (journalists) write publicly. When the form the author uses is narrative, the writing produced becomes a work of literature. Time and again from this point on in the diary Anne speaks openly to herself, even though she continues to begin each entry with the magic rune, 'Dear Kitty'. But then Kitty is nothing other than an aspect, a persona of Anne—herself as her own imagined reader. Kitty is literally and metaphorically the reader in the book.

Assuming Anne's menstrual cycle was fairly normal and even allowing for the irregularity experienced by some girls when they start, her first period must have occurred sometime during or just before the previous November—as it happens, around the time she lost her pen. That pivotal 6 January entry begins on page 159 of the new edition of the diary. The previous 158 pages cover nineteen months—half of 1942 and all of 1943. After the 6 January entry 179 pages cover the seven months of 1944 before Anne and her family are betrayed and taken away. In the seven months after she mentions that her periods have begun Anne writes nearly three times as much as she wrote in all of the previous nineteen months. It is as if the monthly flow of blood released a tidal flow of words. Certainly, when you read the book as you read a novel, in sequence and all of it in a concentrated time, the change is palpable. There is a surge of energy, a new sense of purpose, an astonishing clarity of insight about herself and other people, about life itself.

Then something else happens. On Wednesday 29 March 1944 Anne listens to a Radio Oranje broadcast from London by a Dutch cabinet minister-in-exile, Mr Bolkestein. He announces that after the war a collection will be made of people's private diaries and letters so that future generations will know what the war was like, not only as described by historians and academics but as recorded at the time by ordinary people in the Netherlands. 'Just imagine,' Anne writes immediately after hearing the broadcast, 'how interesting it would be if I were to publish a novel about the Secret Annexe.'

Not letters, not a diary, but a novel. Already the thought is in her head: what she actually wants to be is a novelist. At once she starts editing, cutting, rewriting, even moving entries around in order to achieve the shape, the pattern, the rhythm, the narrative voice, the transformation she wants. She has become a self-conscious author preparing a work of literary art. She begins to turn a documentary record—a piece of journalism—into a literary work, a private act made appropriate for private reading by publication as a book: the ambiguous paradox of a private relationship achieved by making an artefact that is public.

What is the value of reading a book? What does writing and reading a book do that nothing else can do or doesn't do as well? People give many answers to those questions. There is only one I want to offer now, the one that seems to me to be the be-all and end-all of the matter. And to come at it I want to start with the last words Anne wrote in her diary, on Tuesday 1 August 1944, three days before the raid on the secret annexe by the German Security Police and their Dutch Nazi accomplices.

Anne wasn't happy that day; she was suffering a bout of typical adolescent confusion. She begins the entry by saying that she's 'a bundle of contradictions'. But what does 'contradiction' mean? she asks. 'Like so many words, it can be interpreted in two ways,' and she goes on to ponder the different meanings. Then she accuses herself of being two people, one who is superficial and always wins over the other, 'purer, deeper and finer' Anne. She teases herself with the thought that people don't like her. Yet, she says, 'I know exactly how I'd like to be, how I am . . . on the inside.' And a few lines later she writes that she keeps on 'trying to find a way to become what I'd like to be, and what I could be if . . . if only there were no other people in the world'.

These were the last words she wrote. They sound across the bleak years of a terrible century with an almost desolating poignancy. Yet they carry also a saving grace.

If we want to, we can think of that final entry as recording a typical case of teenage angst, which of course it does. Even so, that vulnerable 'if only', standing on the edge of an ellipsis, stares into an abyss. It is important to note that both ellipses in the passage are included in Anne's Dutch manuscript. She intended them. They are not editorial or translators' insertions. What is the meaning of an ellipsis when used like this? A hint of hesitancy? An indication of the writer's uncertainty about how to express what she wants to say? A sign that the writer is not yet clear about her meaning? Her final words seem almost despairing. Did she mean them to be? Had she known, as she could not, that these would be the diary's last words, would she have ended like that? Or would she have preferred to end with the entry just two before the last, the wonderful long entry of 15 July:

> It's utterly impossible for me to build my life on a foundation of chaos, suffering and death. I see the world being slowly transformed into a wilderness, I hear the approaching thunder that, one day, will destroy us too, I feel the suffering of millions. And yet, when I look up at the sky, I somehow feel that everything will change for the better, that this cruelty too will end, that peace and tranquillity will return once more. In the meantime, I must hold to my ideals. Perhaps the day will come when I'll be able to realize them!

No teenage angst here, but an author in full flow, eloquent and mature. We must always keep in mind that so far as Anne is concerned, the diary was never finished. The book we have is work-in-progress. In some ways that's lucky for us, because we see Anne the person in the raw, so to speak, often unguarded, the way one is when talking to oneself. And yes, she is a typical teenager, a bundle of contradictions, who has emotional highs and lows, fights with her sister and her parents, is devoted to her father, a girl who loves reading junky biographies of film stars mixed in with the highest of high literature written not only in German and Dutch and French but in Latin as well, a girl whose favourite school subject is history, who enjoys Greek and Roman mythology, is fascinated by the genealogical charts of the European royal families, and loathes maths, an adolescent who longs to fall in love and who holds passionately articulated views about the liberation of women and their proper place in the world. But typical though she was, she was quite untypical in her ability to see into herself and other people with clarity and wisdom.

Above all she valued her ambition and her gift as a writer. On Wednesday 5 April 1944, she wrote:

I want to go on living even after my death! And that's why I'm so grateful to God for having given me this gift, which I can use to develop myself and to express all that's inside me!

When I write I can shake off all my cares. My sorrow disappears, my spirits are revived! But, and that's a big question, will I ever be able to write something great, will I ever become a journalist or a writer?

I hope so, oh, I hope so very much, because writing allows me to record [recapture] everything, all my thoughts, ideals and fantasies.

We have only one eyewitness account of Anne the author at work. It is by Miep Gies, the selflessly brave office worker who looked after the Franks and the others in the secret annexe. One beautiful hot day in July 1944, less than a month before Anne and her family were betrayed, Miep finished work early and as the office was quiet she decided to pay the Franks an unexpected visit. When she climbed the steep stairs to the hiding place the first thing she saw was Anne alone in the gloomy room at the head of the stairs, sitting at the old kitchen table beside the blacked-out window.

I saw that Anne was writing intently, and hadn't heard me. I was quite close to her and was about to turn and go when she looked up, surprised, and saw me standing there. In our many encounters over the years, I'd seen Anne, like a chameleon, go from mood to mood, but always with friendliness. She'd never been anything but effusive, admiring, and adoring with me. But I saw a look on her face at this moment that I'd never seen before. It was a look of dark concentration, as if she had a throbbing headache. This look pierced me, and I was speechless. She was suddenly another person there writing at the table. I couldn't say a word. My eyes were locked with Anne's brooding ones.

Mrs Frank must have heard me come in, and I heard her soft step beside me. I could tell from the sound of her voice when she finally spoke that she'd summed up the situation. She spoke in German, which she used only when a situation was difficult. Her voice was ironic, and yet kind. 'Yes, Miep, as you know, we have a daughter who writes.'

At this, Anne stood up. She shut the book she was writing in and, with that look still on her face, she said, in a dark voice that I'd also never heard before, 'Yes, and I write about you, too.'

She continued to look at me, and I thought, I must say something; but all I could say, in as dry a tone as I could muster, was, 'That will be very nice.'

I turned and went away. I was upset by Anne's dark mood. I knew that more and more her diary had become her life. It was as if I had interrupted an intimate moment in a very, very private friendship.

Every author will recognize that scene and Anne's 'mood'. What Miep's unexpected appearance interrupted is indeed an intimate and very private friendship. It is the friendship that can exist only in the process of writing and of reading between the author-in-the-book and the reader-in-the-book. Or perhaps, rather than 'friendship', a more appropriate word would be 'companionship', for the relationship between author- and reader-in-the-book can never be—is not meant to be—like the friendship between two people in the everyday sense of that word. To start with, there can be no reciprocity of action. The reader cannot instantly speak back to the author in the conversational way that two friends can speak back to each other in everyday life. They cannot help each other if the car breaks down or they need a baby-sitter for the evening. They cannot take holidays together or share a meal. They cannot be together at all, except in the companionship of the book. And it is a companionship that lives its life only in the part of our being we call our consciousness.

What does 'consciousness' mean? When Anne found herself teetering on the edge of her final ellipsis, pondering what she could be if there were no other people in the world, she was on the hunt for the solution to that question. The fact is she had already found the answer and had written about it sixteen days and only two entries before. As is often the case for authors, the book she was writing revealed to her something she unconsciously already knew.

It was around the time of Miep Gies' surprise visit that Anne wrote the passage I have in mind, the one with which I began. Here it is again, this time in the translation by Susan Massotty.

> I have one outstanding character trait that must be obvious to anyone who's known me for any length of time: I have a great deal of self-knowledge. In everything I do, I can watch myself as if I were a stranger. I can stand across from the everyday Anne and, without being biased or making excuses, watch what she's doing, both the good and the bad. This self-awareness never leaves me, and every time I open my mouth, I think, 'You should have said that differently' or 'That's fine the way it is.' I condemn myself in so many ways that I'm beginning to realize the truth of Father's adage: 'Every child has to raise itself.' Parents can only advise their children or point them in the right direction. Ultimately, people shape their own characters.

All translation is an act of interpretation. Susan Massotty makes three importantly different choices of word from those in the Mooyaart-Doubleday version:
'self-awareness' for 'self-consciousness',
'stranger' for 'outsider',
'never leaves me' for 'haunts me'.

Not only that, Mooyaart-Doubleday flags 'self-consciousness' with inverted commas, whereas Massotty doesn't.

Early in the passage Anne sets the context by using '*zelfkennis*', for which the usual English would be 'self-knowledge'. Massotty uses it, though rather awkwardly; Mooyaart-Doubleday prefers the more everyday and fluent expression 'my knowledge of myself'. Anne then writes about how she can watch herself and her behaviour as if she '*een vreemde was*': was someone strange, a foreigner or an alien. Strictly, then, Massotty is more accurate than Mooyaart-Doubleday in choosing 'stranger' rather than 'outsider'. But a stranger does not know you at all, whereas an outsider may know you very well but from a point of view neither you nor an insider can have of you. And it is clear from the context that Anne's '*vreemde*' knows her very well. So Mooyaart-Doubleday's choice may be fitter to the spirit of Anne's meaning.

Which brings us to the sentence in which the translators use either 'self-awareness' or 'self-consciousness' for the Dutch '*zelfgevoel*'. Though the dictionary translates it as 'self-esteem', '*zelfgevoel*' more accurately means 'being sensitive to, or having a sensitive feeling for oneself'. The passage doesn't support 'self-esteem' as being true to the drift of Anne's thought, and 'this sensitive feeling for myself' would be an awkward bodge. Mooyaart-Doubleday decides that what Anne actually means is best covered by 'self-consciousness', but flags the uncertainty that this is precisely what Anne meant by marking the word with inverted commas. This left Massotty in a dilemma familiar to translators. Should she accept her predecessor's decision at this contentious point or find another solution? Her instinct must have been to find another solution. After all, why retranslate a text if one simply follows one's predecessor whenever there is a possibility of another way of expressing the original? So she chooses 'self-awareness' as an acceptable synonym, and flags no caution, perhaps thinking that inverted commas would be read as Anne's doing, not the translator's. After all, translators often make choices between one word and another without highlighting the choice when the original cannot be equalled by one word in the host language.

This intimate knowledge of herself, this '*zelfgevoel*', Anne says, never 'lets go' of her for one moment. The sense of the Dutch is of being held in the grip of something, almost of being captured or trapped by it. What Anne is talking about is the experience of constantly observing yourself as if this observant 'you' were like another, invisible being, one who inhabits the 'you' who speaks and behaves, an other you who haunts you and from whom you cannot escape. Massotty's choice of 'never leaves me' is literally accurate but less apt and telling than Mooyaart-Doubleday's preference for 'haunted by'.

Throughout, Massotty's is the more literal, more narrowly accurate version, Mooyaart-Doubleday's the more fluent, more eloquent, more guided by a judgement about the spirit, the underlying sense—the subtext—of Anne's words. Which one best represents the nature of Anne's text I'm not sufficiently proficient in Dutch to judge. But I prefer Mooyaart-Doubleday's as a piece of English prose, and feel it to be more like Anne's English would have been, a precocious girl writing in her second language in the 1940s, than Massotty's, which has been given the sound, the tone, the diction, the sentence structure of a modern teenage American girl using her mother tongue.

As well as the language, look at the paragraphing as another sign of this. Anne's often long, now-seeming 'old fashioned' paragraphs, in which she often encloses dialogue, have been broken by Massotty into shorter paragraphs, and the dialogue separated out in the conventional manner of contemporary journalistic fiction. No doubt this was a deliberate decision by translator and publisher to try to make the book more appealing and contemporary to young readers today. But the question has to be asked: Does this treatment properly represent the cast of Anne's mind—her way of thinking, the shape of her consciousness? Or does it remake her into a different person? I think it does. The Anne of the 1952 version is not the same Anne who inhabits the 1995 translation. This is a problem in all translation, and is the main reason why we need more than one translation—or a new one every twenty years or so—of every book that matters.

Why do we read the writing we call literature? For the plot, the story, the characters, the ideas, the information, the language, the descriptions of settings, the humour...what? Each of these and more, perhaps, depending on the book.

We can best come to the heart of the matter by asking another question. Why do I read the books of a kind I would never ever usually read? I can only answer for myself. For example, I do not like books that are full of long descriptions of the countryside, and itemize every detail of their characters' clothing. Yet I am devoted to the novels of Iris Murdoch, which are full of such passages. Why do her books engage me? Because I am fascinated by the being who inhabits the books: the mind and spirit that inform everything in them, so that even the long passages of description silence my bias and hook my attention. This is a consciousness with whom I am happy to keep company no matter what she is writing about. She may tire me, but she never bores me; she may puzzle me but I always feel the difficulty is worth making an effort to understand; she constantly unsettles my complacency about myself, yet in a way that leaves me asking for more. In sum, she enlivens me.

What do I mean by 'consciousness'? Here is one answer to that tricky question in a rabbinical definition.

Consciousness is
the urgency of a destination to the Other
and not an eternal return to self,
an innocence without stupidity,
an absolute uprightness which is also absolute self-criticism,
  read in the eyes of the one who is the goal of my uprightness
  and whose look calls me into question.
It is a movement toward the Other that does not come back to
  its point of origin in the way that diversion comes back,
  incapable of transcendence—
a movement beyond anxiety and stronger than death.

At the root of our cultural history is the understanding that we know who we are and what we are by paying close attention, not to the self, but to the Other. This Other, as Anne learned, can be an inner self who observes and criticizes.

A book presents us with the Other who is the author-in-the-book, as the Other whose company I keep in the novels of Iris Murdoch engages my mind in such a way that I reflect differently on myself so that by the end I am not where I was at the beginning—a movement that does not return to its point of origin.

In our everyday, extra-book life, the Other is the loved person who eyes me and whose look calls me into question.

At the intellectual mid point between this primary Hebraic understanding and our own times comes René Descartes' famous assertion, 'I think, therefore I am.' Nowadays, we know this is incomplete, for it misses out the understanding that the rabbinical definition shows to be essential. I made a restatement of this for myself after reading Ludwig Wittgenstein and trying to understand what that utterly modern post-Einstein philosopher was getting at.

I think, therefore I am.
I am, therefore I am observed.

And this, of course, is a philosophical palindrome: I am observed, therefore I am. I am, therefore, I think.

Why do little children love to play peek-a-boo? Because in the flux between being seen and not being seen they are playing out the fact of their existence. To be seen is to exist, not to be seen is not to exist. And in the game it matters greatly who sees you and who you see. It is not a game you play with an enemy.

Literature is an elaborate, serious version of peek-a-boo. The basis of it is story. All cultures, non-literate as well as literate, have a great repertoire of stories, just as every individual, literate or not, has a memory full of them. They haunt us, they play us, they read us, they tell us, they make us. Without them we are nothing. We do not exist. We are the stories we tell. And in our present culture we exist individually and as a species only through the stories we write down. Today we are defined and legitimized by print, not by word-of-mouth. This I know, and this is all I know for sure.

Because book-writing, by which I mean literary writing, is the best means by which we express what is innermost, and because book-reading leaves the entire act of interpretation to the reader's inner self, we not only come intimately closer to the consciousness of another person than is possible in any other way but are also engaged with our own consciousness more intricately and more actively than by any other means. This is why we so often feel when we have read a great book, a book that matters to us, that we have grown, that we are more aware of some aspect of our self, of other people, of life itself, than we were before. It is why, in adolescence especially but throughout life, certain books are an epiphany, a showing forth, that help us know who we are and what we are and what we can be.

To put it like this is, of course, to make a religious statement. It is certainly to make of serious (as against pastime) book-reading a spiritual act of worship and of prayer. This is something Anne Frank, a Jew, would have known. Or, to put it in George Steiner's words from his book *No Passion Spent*:

> The disciplines of reading, the very idea of close commentary and interpretation, textual criticism as we know it, derive from the study of Holy Scripture or, more accurately, from the incorporation and development in that study of older practices of

> Hellenistic grammar, recension and rhetoric. [. . .] [O]ur criticisms of texts, our endeavours to pass from letter to spirit, are the immediate heirs to the textualities of western Judaeo-Christian theology and biblical-patristic exegetics.

We may no longer believe in an identifiable God, we may not have faith in any of the old religions. But this we cannot deny, that writing and reading have always to do with recognition. Recognition. Re-cognition. Re-knowing. Knowing with self-conscious awareness something we did not know we already knew.

It has always seemed magical that a few abstract signs—in our case the twenty-six letters of the alphabet and a few signs we call punctuation—can create within us such variety, and in their infinite combinations wrapped into a book can bring to life a knowledge of ourselves and a power over ourselves that cannot be gained by any other means. Writing-and-reading forges that connection, and is at the same time a celebration of our self-creative power.

The truth about Anne Frank's pen is that it helped make her what she is. Not what she was, which is something we can never know. But what she *is*—an ever-present being, a consciousness who lives and breeds as long as someone else, someone Other, can read what she wrote, and by complete attention become her.

All of a Tremble to See His Danger

The Adventures of Huckleberry Finn first appeared over one hundred years ago. Hard to believe it's that old. Many books written since then—*Catcher in the Rye*, for example, which owes its inspiration to Huck—seem so much more dated, not half so alive and fresh. Reading it again, I realized just how much it has taught me, and goes on teaching me. About adolescence and the things that matter most at that time of life; about how to tell stories; about how to read and how not to; and about the function of adolescent literature as a metaphor, a way by which we examine the social, moral, political and spiritual questions of our time.

For me, what in North America is called young adult, and in Britain teenage, literature is not simply *for* adolescents. It is written on behalf *of* them too, so might better be called the literature of youth. By which I mean it represents the adolescent view of life to young people and to adults alike. Youth literature is not, to my mind, a ghetto intended for and restricted to those who live in that patch. Nor is it a genre, for it includes work in many genres, such as detective stories and science fiction, romances whether of the sentimental or the fantastic kind, realistic novels about contemporary life, poetry, plays, and so on. Its central concern is the adolescent experience, and its depiction of adolescence becomes an image for, a metaphor of, the whole of life. The result should be a book in which both adolescent and adult readers mutually find significant meaning for their own lives.

It is on these topics that I'd like to dwell rather than on *Huckleberry Finn*, but I'll view them through the eyes of that proto-adolescent Huck Finn. I have headed each chapter of this short story about today's youth literature with some of Huck's words, sayings of such pith and moment that they reach across the intervening century without any loss of pertinence.

It was like being born again,
I was so glad to find out who I was

It is a truism that adolescence is a time of seeking for an identity, and that the literature written for and of adolescents explores that experience as much as or more than any other. Huck is right: when you find out who you are, it is like being born again. And this phrase tells us something that present-day literature for the young often omits, or at any rate neglects. The experience of finding out who you are is not simply a matter of emotion or intellect or the social and political constraints and frustrations of the society you happen to live in. Rather, it is spiritual in nature, encompassing other aspects of life and transcending them.

One of the problems for a writer of youth literature these days is to know how to deal with spiritual experience. Years ago, when people conventionally believed in a God they could agree about, acceptable patterns of stories about spiritual experience were easy to come by. Now, when there is dispute about whether there are any gods at all, never mind agreement about one, those patterns are threadbare and faded. Finding a way to make a convincing narrative about spiritual truth is therefore one of the challenges that face us. Some of our best writers for the young are finding metaphors that work. The American Virginia Hamilton is one example; Australian Patricia Wrightson is another; Alan Garner is achieving it in my country.

When I look at *Huckleberry Finn* to find out how Mark Twain dealt with spiritual experience, I am astonished and delighted again by the relevance of his methods to our needs today. In Twain's time the agreed spiritual formulas were still usable, but he not only rejects them and does something else, he turns his solution into a critique of the conventional modes. So the first thing he teaches any writer about the craft of writing of youth is this: Look at what is currently being written and regarded as acceptable, and turn it on its head. That way you'll strike closer to the truth.

How does Twain do this? First, he has Huck adopted by the Widow Douglas, whose benevolent determination to improve him finds expression in the conventional religious instruction of the day. She promises Huck his dearest desires now and a heavenly life after death if he learns to pray, reads his Bible and does as he's told. He tries it and it doesn't seem to work, but he's a long-suffering boy and tolerant, so he assumes it is his own fault, not the Widow's. Then Miss Watson is introduced into the household, a woman of a spiky, unhuggable nature whose main concern is to improve Huck's social manners by threatening him with hell. Huck finds this less than appealing but survives by salving himself with his wit. It is the violent affection of his natural father that finally drives him from the Widow's shelter and onto the river and into the company of Miss Watson's fugitive slave, Jim.

In other words, Twain begins with everyday life as most young people knew it and, by force of circumstances over which his adolescent protagonist has no control, brings Huck into a situation that faces him with the central questions of his own personality and of the society of his day. Huck is trying to escape from adult requirements, whether well-intentioned or ill-, and to opt for the irresponsibility of childhood. But in attempting his escape he is thrown into company with another escapee, a man oppressed by one of the most insistent social and political, not to say moral, problems, of the time, the black slave Jim.

After that, the story of Huck's adolescence is inextricably mixed up with the story of Jim. This is plot-making of the most elegant kind in which all the threads of the narrative, whether of action, character, theme or setting (to use the grid of Arnoldonian criticism), are integrated into a coherent, resonant whole. For the adolescent truth to which Mark Twain is giving shape is this: in order to know who you are, you have to be free to become who you wish to be. The central concern of adolescence, therefore, is freedom-to-be.

Robert Cormier's *The Chocolate War* is a good example of the same technique at work. He sets his story in a Roman Catholic boys' school run by monks, where you would expect the spiritual values of life to be high on the agenda, gives the bullies the run of the place, and inspires one boy to stand against the mob. This is *Tom Brown's Schooldays* stood on its head; it is the Jesus story re-worked in a twentieth-century school where Christ is supposed to be the ideal and guide; it is a paradigm of the greatest political evil of our day—the evil of state-organized (or condoned) crime against individuals who in the end have no power against it but the strength of their spirit, which means the strength that comes from confidence in your own death. Yet *The Chocolate War* is entirely about adolescence; Cormier's book succeeds because it speaks convincingly and significantly on behalf of the state of being which teenaged Jerry Renault explores for us.

Jerry learns that you get to know who you want to be by obtaining the freedom-to-be. Huck learns that too. When he says that finding out who he is was like being born again, his words are laden, as they often are, with a complicated irony. At the time, near the end of the book, he is searching for Jim, who is locked up on the Phelpses' farm. Huck arrives and is greeted, he knows not why, like a long-lost brother. He plays for time, hoping to find out who the Phelpses think he is. At last they let the name slip. They think he is Tom Sawyer. And to Huck, knowing this is such a relief it is like being born again.

Here we have another instance of what has happened throughout the book: Huck's identity is imposed on him by the adults on whom he depends. To the Widow Douglas he is a dutiful adopted son, to the Grangerfords he is the recently orphaned offspring of a respectable Arkansas farmer, on one occasion he even pretends he is a girl. All this role-play, this enforced trying on of parts, is turned into a theatrical image during one of the longest sequences in the book when Huck becomes stagehand, bit-part player and apprentice to the King and the Duke in their bogus theatre, the sole purpose of which is to defraud innocent people of their material possessions. A century ago your material possessions were often called your substance, a word that in our day and in Mark Twain's might also mean the essence of one's being. In other words, the soul. Hard to think of a more tightly constructed metaphor.

Every adolescent has to deal with the realization that, so far in life, his or her identity has been imposed by adults. Breaking free from these impositions is one of the struggles of that phase. In order to achieve freedom adolescents begin by trying to shrug off the identities given them as children. They often attack the orthodox social and psychological categories assigned to them by society, seeing in these simply another imposition. Instead, they demand an authority based on their own uniqueness, and on their individual revision of established laws and customs. They become discomforting spiritual visionaries, holding out ideals of freedom and behaviour we should all live by. And because of the way they assert themselves they often sound like political revolutionaries, which is why many adults feel there is something subversive about even the best-behaved adolescents.

The comic side of this manifestation is that usually it is all talk. At no time are we more loquacious than during adolescence. Never are our thoughts more vaultingly ambitious. Never are we so capable of unsparing honesty. And yet never are our lives so little conducted through action. All adolescents pretend to adults, and even to each other, that just the opposite is the case. And they constantly hunt for significant action in which to involve themselves, the kind of action that will give honourable expression to their visionary ambitions.

In *The Adolescent Idea: Myths of Youth and the Adult Imagination* the American critic Patricia Meyer Spacks traces this very line in literature written since the eighteenth century on behalf of adults. She demonstrates how adolescents as individuals 'suffer uncertainty, absence of power'. Characters like Salinger's Holden Caulfield and Doris Lessing's Martha Quest epitomize 'two typical adolescent manifestations: the need of the young person to invent himself or herself, and the problematic relation of reality and fantasy in youthful experience'.

Perhaps I quote that particular sentence because it appeals to my own experience and bears on my work as an author. My youth novels, from *Breaktime* on, explore just what 'the need of the young person to invent himself or herself' actually means. How do we invent ourselves and what does it feel like? We all know there are conflicts between our fantasies about ourselves and the reality that confronts us. But how do we deal with them? My protagonists showed me just how true it is, as Spacks says, that adolescence is 'a crucial period of ambiguous potential', that we live then in a constant condition of desire, the kind of desire that 'supplies energy, generates conflict, makes action—the stuff of novels. It also raises questions of value'. The deeper I explored beneath the surface of the narrative of each of my first two books, the more I kept stubbing my intellectual toes on the fact that once you begin to grapple with questions of human value you are dealing with matters of the spirit. So my own novels, never mind my reading of other people's, forced me to a reconsideration of spiritual experience and the narrative problems raised by telling a story about it, given the nature of the society we live in, and I tried to confront these directly in the third book, *Now I Know*.

All right then, I'll go to hell

The search for an identity is certainly a central concern of adolescence, but one of the many interesting things about Huck Finn is that he doesn't seem to suffer much in the way of an identity crisis. He doesn't moon around for hours on end wondering who on earth he is. Perhaps the reason is that most adolescents, though searching for an identity, don't have crises about it. After all, in order to have an identity crisis you must already have an identity to have a crisis about. Surely, it is middle-aged people who have identity crises, not adolescents? And like many people in a crisis they tend to project their problems onto those whom they envy or dislike, feel threatened by or want help from, or love enough to feel secure with.

Which explains a lot about the adolescent characters who appear in fiction written on behalf of adults. Spacks shows how they are used to make statements about adult, mostly middle-aged concerns rather than about adolescence itself, finishing her book with these words:

> The young embody our most profound vulnerabilities and our most intimate strengths. They speak to us of our past and of our future. We can imagine them as licensed transgressors, surrogates for ourselves, or as prophets of salvation [. . .] The mythology of adolescence, recorded in fiction [. . .] tells us of ourselves, our ancestors, and our descendants.

In the literature of adulthood we exploit adolescence as a critical viewpoint from which to look at ourselves and reassess what we are and still might be. In some fiction adolescence is merely used to confirm an adult's prejudices about the world, as I think is the case in Anthony Burgess's novel *The Clockwork Orange*, which presents much more the hell-on-earth created by middle-aged men than a world desired by teenagers. Its clash of fantasy and reality tells us more about Burgess and his contemporaries than about adolescence, and is a good example of how adult writers employ adolescent characters to arouse and shift their generation's guilt.

Throughout Spacks's book, though she deals with this subject in literature from the eighteenth century to the present, there is not one mention of *Huckleberry Finn*. Understandable, if it is considered a novel for young readers only. But also perhaps it was ignored because it requires a definition of the difference between the adult exploitation of youth in literature and literature written on behalf of youth, a distinction most literary critics are not prepared to make. They prefer to think that there is no difference, that books published for young readers are simply diminished versions of fiction written for adults. Even a critic of such note as T.S. Eliot can only allow himself to call *Huckleberry Finn* a masterpiece, which he does in his Introduction to the Cresset edition, by claiming that it 'does not fall into the category of juvenile fiction'. Did Eliot really think a book could not be both a masterpiece of world literature and a fiction for young readers? And could it be that, like so many academic critics, he did not understand the concept of writing on behalf of a state of life that still lives inside you, even though you are past the age when it is the socially acceptable and psychologically pertinent expression of your existence?

In other words, I am saying that though I am presently enjoying the pleasures and pains associated with middle age, there is still alive inside me the state of being I experienced as a sixteen-year-old adolescent. I do not simply mean I remember that time, and look back at it with whatever degree of nostalgia or distaste my present personality dictates. Rather, I mean that adolescence still informs me, is still active in me. Just as my childhood is. And I am glad. Indeed, one of the values that distinguishes the best literature of childhood and youth is that it helps maintain and refresh those states within us. That is part of their purpose as literary forms, one of the reasons we need them, whether or not we are professionally involved. Childhood and youth are not the sole possessions of children and adolescents.

I think Mark Twain discovered this through his own writing. *The Adventures of Tom Sawyer* is a book about boyhood written by an adult looking back at his experience of it. Twain knew this, which is why he told William Howells: 'It's *not* a boy's book, at all. It will only be read by adults. It is only written for adults'. He was wrong about boys not reading it because he wasn't allowing for the fact that many children are quite as capable of entering into the adult view of themselves as adults are of re-entering childhood, if the fiction enables them to do so, which Tom does. But he was right about it being a book written on behalf of adults. The narrator's tone of voice puts years between the storyteller and his protagonist, as I think the quotation I've used on page 45 shows.

My author's intuition—I have no other evidence to go on—tells me he almost at once felt uneasy about what he had done. In a sense, and to couch what I'm trying to say in crude shorthand, he had betrayed his boyhood, warped what it had been and what it had meant, by making use of it, perhaps for nostalgic, perhaps for commercial reasons. At any rate, I fancy the emotional pressure was strong in him to make amends. Besides, he was not an entirely happy man around the time *Tom Sawyer* was written. The small-town boy from the frontier life of Missouri had settled for the old-world habits of the cultural establishment of New England and had cut himself off from his roots. He was playing a part he was neither born into nor suited for—cause enough for a middle-aged identity crisis.

It was the honesty of the man that provoked him to write *Huckleberry Finn*. He could have put *Tom Sawyer* behind him, suppressing the sense of guilt about his betrayal. Plenty of writers work that trick and survive happily enough, but no author can. As I try to explain elsewhere [pages 13-14], writers make books of whatever kind their readers want—they are reader-focused. If readers want nostalgic tales of childhood, a writer can supply them. But authors don't do that—they are text-focused. They have to discover what the book they are impelled to write wants to be. Likewise, their readers have to give themselves to the finished work and discover how it wants to be read. Authors work according to the truth of their experience, and if they deliberately warp it they lose the self-respect of their vocation.

Mark Twain was at first a writer, hacking out copy for newspapers and the popular press. But he found himself as an author and then wanted to reveal the truth he knew in the form of the best fictional modes he could conceive. By the time he wrote *Tom Sawyer* this was the crisis of his life, the moment when he finally chose his identity. He was one of those people whose adolescence extends long into adulthood, because it is not until then that they meet the experience that shifts their state of being. The result in Twain was that he authored *Huckleberry Finn*, from which, according to Ernest Hemingway, comes all modern American literature. Willa Cather lists it as one of the three American books she feels have the possibility of a long, long life. T.S. Eliot is not alone among critics in calling it a masterpiece, and numerous authors, including James Joyce, have acknowledged owing it a debt.

Twain's adolescent crisis, suffered in middle age, gave us this wonder, the first great book written on behalf of youth, the prototype for young adult literature, a sampler of craft skill, a progenitor of scores of books since. Lionel Trilling says that its greatness lies 'primarily in its power of telling the truth'. He is also one of the few critics who acknowledges that an essential part of its greatness is 'that it succeeds first as a boys' book'. It tells the truth about being an adolescent—not an adult-reflecting truth, but truth as an adolescent sees it. And it does even more. While honouring his youth, the author takes with him into his novel the knowledge of life he has acquired since, and transposes it by his craft skill into knowledge that a teenager can discover.

In Twain's case, this was achieved by investing the whole of his self in Huck. The unhappy man suffering a middle-aged crisis is really describing himself when Huck says, on the first page of the novel, 'I couldn't stand it no longer, I lit out. I got into my old rags [...] and was free and satisfied.' A sentence later Tom Sawyer drags him back with promises of a different kind of satisfaction, but by chapter three Huck knows it won't do: 'all that stuff was just [...] Tom Sawyer's lies' he tells us, and runs for freedom.

This is, as I say, crude shorthand. Authors of fiction are always both more and less than their characters. Scott Fitzgerald is right when he says somewhere in his Notebooks: 'There never was a good biography of a good novelist. There couldn't be. He is too many people.' And anyhow, what has this to do with Huck's decision to go to hell?

The moment of his alarming choice occurs near the end of the book. In order to understand its significance and why the religious imagery has an ironic reach that exceeds its colloquial grasp, we must recall what is happening at the time. Huck is agonizing over his friendship with Jim and has just written a letter to Miss Watson, telling her where she can find her slave. He does this because he can think of no other way to save Jim from being sold to strangers. He has even tried kneeling down and promising to give up sin if God will lend a hand. But that doesn't work; he can't even say the words. He knows why: 'My heart warn't right [. . .] I warn't square [. . .] I was playing double.' Betrayal is the problem again. So the letter to Miss Watson is a desperate attempt to set himself square by doing his socially conditioned duty. But that doesn't work either. He recalls all he and Jim have done together, and knows that to give Jim away to Miss Watson or to anyone else would be the greatest betrayal of all: the betrayal of their common humanity, never mind what the customary laws of society might demand. He looks at the letter and realizes that for the first time in his life, 'I'd got to decide, for ever, betwixt two things.'

I mentioned earlier the desire adolescents feel for involvement in significant action. Huck now finds out what it means when that desire becomes a reality. It is the moment when a young person realizes that the power needed to bring idealistic vision into touch with active reality lies at last in their grasp. This is the most testing crisis of adolescence, a crisis of choice between possibilities of what you might be, and finding at the same moment that each possibility bears the potential of a terrible cost. Huck's choice dramatizes the dilemma at its most stark. If he chooses to give Jim away, his reward will be the comfort of approbation from the controlling establishment, but it will also mean the finally cruel and self-despising comfort of weakness, for thereafter he will be a creature who must settle for the world as he finds it. But to act on the choice, as he puts it, of 'stealing Jim from slavery' and the reality of his action could be the discomfiture of a kind of hell. In Huck's case, it would be the hell of imprisonment by men here on earth and the prophecy of those same men that he will suffer the Devil's hell in the hereafter.

In Huck, in the decision he must make about his relationship with Jim, the crisis of all adolescents who seek their freedom-to-be meets head on the crisis of freedom in the society of his day. No earthly law or custom is much use at that moment. Everything depends on your view of your own death, what it means to you and what it portends. Is your vision, is your choice worth dying for? That's why Huck's words are so precise and why in the end this insignificant boy's journey down the mighty Mississippi with an insignificant slave is a spiritual odyssey of universal proportions. As we watch him make the choice, we are, in his own words, 'all of a tremble to see his danger'.

The elegance of narrative and irony here is astonishing. Twain so builds his story that from start to finish every episode is a meditation on freedom. Which can be put another way, not in Huck's words this time:

> You wouldn't a ben here
> 'f it hadn't a ben for Jim

Human freedom is always conditional. My freedom depends upon someone else's; so does everyone's. Mark Twain explores some of those conditions.

Jim and Huck personify two extremes. In Jim we see the conditions of other people's freedom at their most cruel. He is not only a slave, he is a fugitive slave, a state of being in which there is even less freedom than the little he would enjoy as a law-abiding captive. He daren't show his face in public for fear of arrest, he can't live in what passes for his own home, nor be with his family. He is a slave in hiding, ever on the run, subject to the whim of anyone who stumbles across him, even other slaves. Huck, on the other hand, is the nearest anyone can get to being a free-roaming spirit. He can do whatever he likes, restricted only by the limits of his own wit and cunning. He even has money to help him—the money he banked with Judge Thatcher after the adventure with Tom Sawyer recounted in the earlier book. But there is one condition that confines him, whether he likes it or not: the birthright of his sonship. Huck cannot escape his parentage until he comes to terms with it.

At the start Huck plays at being the son of Widow Douglas, but that's just a game. He knows he can give up the part whenever he wants. Then his biological father turns up, claims him back, takes him to his shack and locks him in—a literal image of the emotional and psychological truth of a relationship from which he cannot simply walk away.

Huck escapes his father's deadly clutches by digging his way out of the entombing shack, another action which resonates symbolically. In the very next chapter he falls in with Jim and remains with him for the rest of the book. Why does he do this, when associating with Jim threatens his physical freedom in every way? For the simple reason that Huck invests in Jim the conditions of fatherhood. Thereafter, he serves his apprenticeship as a son to the fugitive. Lionel Trilling makes the appealing suggestion that the boy and the slave 'form a family, a primitive community—and it is a community of saints'. (We must be careful here to read 'primitive' not in the debased sense of 'crude and uncivilized' but in the correct sense of 'belonging to the first, the original'.)

Trilling's spiritual language is accurate and appropriate. Jim is more of a good father than Huck's biological father ever was, sustaining him, providing for him, saving him from mortal and emotional danger. (Jim it is, you'll recall, who rescues Huck from drowning and finds the rotting corpse of Huck's dead father and keeps the boy from the trauma of seeing it, or even knowing about it until the very last page of the book.) In every sense, Jim is *in loco parentis* to Huck. But it is Huck who maintains this condition by remaining with Jim, by protecting him, and by aiding Jim's escape, just as a good son would do, even though he knows that by doing so he puts his own life in jeopardy.

No wonder then that when Huck is suffering the final crisis of his adolescence and is trying to persuade himself to give Jim up—give him up in the legal worldly sense and give him up in the spiritual sense of betraying his sonship—he tells us how he

> got to thinking over our trip down the river; and I see Jim before me all the time, in the day, and in the night-time, sometimes moonlight, sometimes storms, and we a-floating along, talking, and singing, and laughing. But somehow I couldn't seem to strike no places to harden me against him, but only the other kind [...] how good he always was.

This is not only a simple description of their life together on the river, it is a lyric account of the spiritually healed state of Huck's being brought about by his relationship with Jim. In more ways than one it is true that, without Jim, Huck wouldn't have been alive. For Jim brings into focus not one main concern of adolescence but two. Freedom is the first; the second is a concern with parents, and especially the crisis between father and son. Jim embodies both. For Huck to obtain his spiritual freedom and gain the self-respect that will allow him to be the man he wants to be, not only must he help Jim obtain his freedom from slavery but he must also resolve his dependence upon, his prejudices about, the legacy of his parent. He must lay to rest the brutality inherited from his bestial, unregenerate biological father. It is not by accident that Twain gives Hamlet's 'To be, or not to be' to the Duke to mangle in front of Huck and Jim during rehearsals for the Nonesuch Theatre. Indeed, Huck is, to use another Shakespearean image, like a son of Caliban who rejects his natural father and adopts Prospero to godfather him into a new life he has chosen for himself. No writer has explored this aspect of adolescent experience more subtly, or more intricately than Mark Twain in *Huckleberry Finn*, and few have succeeded so memorably. Moreover, he works his magic without spoiling the book with what Huck calls:

All the marks of a Sunday school

The family of literature for young readers has its own parentage to live out. It was born of a humble, well-intentioned mother called Simple Didactics, and was sired by a cunning and aggressive father called Cheap Commerce. Many children of these parents inherited the worst of genes from both sides. Even now, they stick close to home and carry on the business of telling readers what to think in off-the-shelf stories more notable for the craftiness of their marketing than the skill of their crafting. *Huckleberry Finn*, however, inherited the best genes from both sides and established a new dynasty. Denying the impulse to tell people *what* to think, Mark Twain designed instead a story that helps young people discover *how* to think. Huck is a full-blown character but he is also a representative of his readers. Huck's story is composed of a sequence of images for his readers to think with alongside him.

Nowhere, for example, is slavery polemically condemned. Instead the novel presents images of slavery: Jim's racial and social slavery; Huck's slavery to identities imposed upon him; the slavery of other characters, like Miss Watson, to conventional behaviour.

The plot is composed of variations on capture and escape. Even the Mississippi is part of this pattern. The river, as Lionel Trilling puts it, 'a road that moves', is Huck and Jim's route to freedom, and yet they are bound to it. Sitting on their floating home, the escapees are safe from their would-be human owners but are prisoners of the dispassionate river, which takes them where it will, once, at a vital moment, carrying them past the point where, by leaving it, Jim would have gained his release.

The river holds them captive and it also captivates them. Huck is only ever truly himself, the person who will live inside the man he wishes to become, when he is drifting down the river, observing the natural world, talking and laughing with Jim and thinking his thoughts. It is on one such happy occasion that he says to Jim, 'this is nice. I wouldn't want to be no-where else but here' and receives Jim's truth-telling reply, 'Well, you wouldn't a ben here, 'f it hadn't a ben for Jim.'

Rather than tell us, Sunday-school fashion, what all this means, Twain leaves us to think it out for ourselves. The images are vividly there to think with: the river that carries to freedom by holding captive; the free-roaming white boy at home on a drifting raft with his surrogate father, a black slave; Huck's pleasure in his wellbeing; Jim's one line of dialogue to make active the potentials of meaning. And not merely one meaning, but many, some of them ironically paradoxical.

Twain works like this all the way through the story, which is why I say that it has so much to tell us about how to read and how not to. When the novel first appeared, its challenge to readers to resolve the indeterminate meanings for themselves led the Sunday-school kind of reader—the kind who wants to be told what to think—to attack it for its 'very low grade morality', as the Concord, Mass., library committee so famously phrased it, as well as for its 'systematic use of bad grammar and an employment of rough, coarse, inelegant expressions'. Which brings me, in-

evitably, to the claims that *Huckleberry Finn* is racially offensive.
Even as I write this, one of our leading poets, Adrian Mitchell, has published a letter in *The Listener*, complaining that the book is

> far worse than offensive, it is poisonous.
>
> Imagine what a black child must feel when the book—with its 200 uses of the word [nigger]—is read aloud in class: 'Whenever *that word* is read out, the other kids stare at me and some of them grin.'
>
> Now *Huckleberry Finn* is a great novel. And Mark Twain was one of the foremost champions of black people in the 19th century [. . .] But he couldn't foresee what the word 'nigger' would become. If we lived in a society of racial harmony, it would be easy. A little historical explanation of the use of the word would precede a reading to a class and all would be well. But we live in an England where racial attacks are commonplace [. . .]
>
> I believe that if Mark Twain were faced with a class of black and white children in England or the States today [...] he would read *Huck Finn* aloud but he would change the word 'nigger' to 'black man', 'black woman', 'black child' [...] I'd like to see a new edition based on such tiny but important substitutions.

The challenge to readers is as serious as ever. What the Concord library objection a hundred years ago and Adrian Mitchell's of today make starkly obvious is how disturbing even sophisticated readers find a combination of irony and the demotic—the everyday speech of everyday people.

To start with, Twain certainly knew about the word 'nigger'. It was poisonous in his day and was always meant to be. That's why he uses it so pointedly, as in the much-quoted exchange between Sally Phelps and Huck '" . . . anybody hurt?" "No'm. Killed a nigger." "Well, it's lucky; because sometimes people do get hurt."' As Huck says in another context, 'Human beings *can* be awful cruel to one another.' To miss the irony in such passages is to seriously misread the book. Try imposing the 'tiny' substitutions Mitchell suggests and the point becomes clear: '"anybody hurt?" "No'm. Killed a black man." "Well, it's lucky; because sometimes people do get hurt." ' The moral impact, if not lost, is certainly rendered banal. Change the word and you might as well lose the entire passage.

Leaving aside for now what should and should not be done in classrooms, about which I'd have a lot to say on another occasion, what I must say here is that for a poet, who deals in irony, to suggest that the irony that helps make *Huck* into the masterpiece he acknowledges it is should be neutered by the removal of one of the words that point up the irony I find distressing. Another version of wanting literature to tell us what to think instead of enabling us to think for ourselves, and dealing with how it is that people come to think as they do.

Twain knew what he was doing; but there is one aspect of his treatment of Jim that, in my estimation, partly explains the charges of racism. It is another irony that it is a weakness within one of the book's great qualities: its innovation with language.

We have to keep in mind that the book's tone is comic. Comic in the sense of being about commonplace people whose story has an optimistic, if you like, 'happy' ending. Comic also in the sense that it incorporates various kinds of wit and humour, from profound ironies to broad jokes. And comic in the sense that it parodies, satirizes and makes fun of every character and every social group who enter its pages. Jim does not escape this treatment, though it has to be conceded that he is much more gently handled than any of the others, including Huck.

Linguistically, most of this comedy takes its cue from the everyday speech of the characters. Ernest Hemingway could say that 'All modern American literature comes from one book by Mark Twain called *Huckleberry Finn*' and not be contradicted because it was the first American novel to raise common people's speech to the level of literature, and not only displayed the vibrant resources of their language but paid it the respect of serious attention. In my view, one of the reasons for the earliest attacks was that the book succeeded. It is perhaps not surprising that the first broadside was fired from the heartland of the New England literary establishment, whose writers took their cue from old England and Europe, where the literary judgement was that the speech of the common people was vulgar, and that the Latin- and Greek-based linguistic manners of the rich and educated were the proper styles for novels and poetry.

Twain had accepted this hegemony. *Tom Sawyer* is written

according to the rules of that game. Here is a sample, the opening of chapter two:

> Saturday morning was come, and all the summer world was bright and fresh, and brimming with life. There was a song in every heart; and if the heart was young the music issued at the lips. There was a cheer in every face, and a spring in every step. The locust trees were in bloom, and the fragrance of the blossoms filled the air [. . .]
>
> Tom appeared on the side-walk with a bucket of white-wash and a long-handled brush. He surveyed the fence, and the gladness went out of nature, and a deep melancholy settled down upon his spirit.

The old guard loved it. There is murder and theft, low life, lying, and irreverence in *Tom Sawyer*, all offences complained of in *Huckleberry Finn*, but no one was upset because they were filtered through the distancing lens of drawing-room discourse. Correct, Latinate grammar, the soothing cadences of familiar polite phrases —'there was a cheer in every face', 'the gladness went out of nature'—and the relaxing knowledge that in the end the narrator will tell you, in suitably amusing fashion, exactly what to think, and that what he tells you to think is exactly what you would wish to think, as indeed he does: 'If [Tom] had been a great and wise philosopher, like the writer of this book, he would now have comprehended that work consists of whatever a body is obliged to do, and that play consists of whatever a body is not obliged to do.'

This is the stuff Mark Twain reacted against in *Huckleberry Finn*. In recovering his youth, in writing on behalf of his adolescent self, he was forced to recover the language of his youth, the language of the people around him then, the frontier people of all classes, whom he put into his story about slavery. For the worst slavery of all is slavery to a language that is not your own. In the language of story we define what we are and invent the identity we want for ourselves. Slaves like Jim knew that better than anyone, which is why they went on making stories, singing songs, and forming a version of English that was their own.

Here, then, is the weakness. Throughout the book Twain tries to use the grammar, syntax, images, diction of the people on whom his characters are based. He warns of this in a prefatory note, explaining that he uses a number of what he calls dialects. He was afraid that his readers, and especially those neighbours of his, the New England literary establishment, would not understand, but rather suppose 'that all these characters were trying to talk alike and not succeeding'. In other words, he was afraid that his readers wouldn't be able to rise to the challenge of knowing how to read a narrative so unfamiliar in its mix of linguistic styles. He was right to worry, as readers down the years have proved time and again.

But this isn't all. He also used phonetically based orthography. And this is the cause of the trouble. If we look at the characters whose speech is spelt phonetically, we see that Judge Thatcher, for example, is treated to none of it, nor is Colonel Sherburn, the man who harangues the lynch mob for their cowardice. No one, in fact, in the upper stratum of society is given anything but conventional grammar and spelling. Tom Sawyer, apart from 'ain't', belongs to this group as well. Huck's speech is unconventionally spelt more often but not to any great extent. The speech of the Phelpses, whatever might be said of their grammar, is conventionally spelled, but not their friends' and neighbours', the farmers and their wives who come to dinner. Which perhaps strikes one as odd, given that they belong to the same locality and are social equals. But there is a difference; the Phelpses' neighbours are figures of fun in the farce of Tom Sawyer's rescue of Jim.

Sorted out like this we see that the lower down the social scale Twain goes and the more he wants to use a character for comic purposes the more he employs phonetically based spelling to represent their speech. (Dickens does something of the same.) Unfortunately Jim is at the furthest extreme of this technique. In his determination to bring Jim's speech into the book with as much accuracy as he could command, attempting to capture its sound as well as style, Twain confused two aims: his aim to investigate his subject matter and his characters through comedy; and his aim to honour the everyday speech of ordinary folk and make literature from it.

The result is that some readers, whether they know why or not, feel Twain is poking malicious fun, is condescending to the socially and educationally least well off, and to Jim in particular. So the white establishment disliked him for the innovation of making common speech equal with their own; and the defenders of Jim criticized him—and still do—for seeming to suggest that black English is a comically uneducated form of establishment white English. That Twain achieved the first is admirable, that phonetically based spelling as a technique for representing speech is a failure is a lesson we can all learn from him.

Some writers still haven't learned it. One who has is Virginia Hamilton. Here she is, doing what Twain was aiming to do, in *The People Could Fly*, her retelling of black slave stories. The passage is the opening of the first story, 'He Lion, Bruh Bear, and Bruh Rabbit'.

> Say that he Lion would get up each and every mornin. Stretch and walk around. He'd roar, 'ME AND MYSELF. ME AND MYSELF,' like that. Scare all the little animals so they were afraid to come outside in the sunshine. Afraid to go huntin or fishin or whatever the little animals wanted to do.
>
> 'What we gone do about it?' they asked one another. Squirrel leapin from branch to branch, just scared. Possum playin dead, couldn't hardly move him.
>
> He Lion just went on, stickin out his chest and roarin, 'ME AND MYSELF. ME AND MYSELF.'

The effect is entirely achieved by a careful choice of diction and rhythm, respect for the grammatical constructions of the language source, and the one unusual orthographic device of dropping the 'g' from the participle, which seems to me as acceptable as the elisions 'don't' and 'can't'. Like other writers, I now often elide 'do you', to 'd'you', in dialogue because it more accurately represents what many people say (as they say 'won't'), and because on the page 'do you' strikes the eye as formal speech.

In Britain sensitive work similar to that of Hamilton in the USA has been achieved by writers like Alan Garner, William Mayne, John Gordon, Jan Mark, Grace Nichols and John Agard, who have all brought demotic forms of English into children's and youth literature, where in the past such accents and dialects were regarded as unliterary comic versions of the language.

Twain led the way in and should be applauded for it.

Equally, he led the way, and still does, in shifting our understanding of the kind of story that can be written for adolescents. What Huck dismisses as bearing all the marks of a Sunday school is a story he has been told by Tom Sawyer. The kind of story Huck Finn likes is quite different. By entwining the two kinds in one book Twain creates something new, something of which, to use Huck's words again, it might be said:

It was a grand adventure and mysterious,
so it hit him where he lived

Huckleberry Finn begins with an intertextual reference: we're told of its connection with *The Adventures of Tom Sawyer*. And in the first four chapters Tom Sawyer tries to arrange another similar escapade for his gang. 'What's the line of business?,' Ben Rogers asks. 'Nothing,' Tom replies, 'only robbery and murder.' (Worth noting that the joke works in exactly the same way as Huck's reply to Mrs Phelps quoted earlier. Here, in a boyishly naive exchange right at the beginning of the novel, we are being prepared for the serious irony to come.)

Huck refers to Tom's book. Tom refers all his adventures to other people's books. When his gang suggest ways of doing things that Tom dislikes, he says they can't 'because it ain't in the books . . . Don't you reckon that the people that made the books knows what's the correct thing to do?' I'm always amused when I remember that at the same time as *Huckleberry Finn* was being finished Robert Louis Stevenson was publishing *Treasure Island*, a story in just the right line of business for Tom Sawyer, but not for Huck. Tom's reality is based on his fantasies about characters he will never meet, who do things he will never do, and who live according to a crudely simple code of good and bad. This is the stuff Huck dismisses as Tom Sawyer's lies that bear all the marks of a Sunday school. So he leaves Tom and follows his own line of business. Huck's reality is based on everyday events that happen to him; indeed, so firmly is his story fixed in life as it was lived in his day that the novel is by many counted a valuable historical document. It tells the truth about life yet manages also to be a grand adventure.

At the end of his own two hundred pages, Huck suffers the climax of his adolescence, the crisis of his relationship with Jim, and makes his life-and-death determining choice. At that moment the story of his adolescence ends and the story of his adulthood begins. At which point Tom Sawyer appears again, and there follows the long final episode when Tom plays out one of his fantasy adventures, only this time the object of his pretence is a real person, a slave.

This ending has often been criticized. Hemingway calls it a cheat. I disagree. Something like it is essential to the structure and manner of the book, and there are a number of reasons why it is as it is. The one important to my argument is that Twain uses the opening and closing Tom Sawyer scenes as a frame for Huck's story. The first chapters set up the conventional action-packed hero fantasy, then Twain uses it against itself, till at the end it descends into farce. That is the importance of the final Tom Sawyer episode. After two hundred pages of Huck's truth, Tom Sawyer's game of let's pretend is ridiculous, even offensive. A clichéd form is fashioned by Twain into something thoughtful and refreshed. Superficial readers like Tom Sawyer are taken on at their own game and are given the chance of becoming readers with a deepened sense of reality. Adolescence is depicted through its own eyes and enabled to think honestly about itself. Adults are observed with a clarity that is critical yet compassionate—a quality most young adult fiction still lacks. He sets up the conventional kind of story written for young people in his day, the Tom Sawyer kind, and in Huck's story shows, first, how it is all lies, and, second, how a story can be told so that it incorporates the truth about life while at the same time being a grand adventure that will hit young readers where they live. The key to his success is in Twain's way of telling: in the absorption of his second self, the implied author, into the protagonist and narrator of the book, Huck Finn; and in his management of narrative form. In both he was innovative.

Huckleberry Finn trusts adolescents with the truth. It doesn't duck the realities of life but acknowledges, indeed reveals how 'sometimes people do get hurt' and how all too often it is 'enough to make a body ashamed of the human race'. But neither is it afraid of the loving, the delicate, the tender and beautiful aspects of life. And because of its irony and variety of humour, it maintains throughout a tone of unsentimental optimism. The last thing it is, in other words, is phony or life-diminishing. True, it doesn't deal with sex, which might be thought a significant lack these days. But, like the handling of Jim's speech, that has to do with the history of its time, just as our endless preoccupation with sex has to do with the history of our own time and may seem unbalanced one hundred years from now.

No period is without its stupidities, no book without its flaws. But the flaws in Twain's novel have as much to teach us as do its strengths. Though I should add, from not a little experience, that anyone trying to live up to the standards set by Twain will certainly be driven to say with Huck Finn, 'if I'd a knowed what a trouble it was to make a book I wouldn't a tackled it.'

Schools in Stories

TALBOT BAINES REED

> Literature as a whole may be considered ... as a laboratory for thought experiments that, thanks to the mediation of reading, we may apply to ourselves. *Paul Ricoeur*
>
> The act of getting a story or a novel published is an act of communication, an attempt to impose one's personality and beliefs on other people. *Doris Lessing*
>
> You write in order to change the world, knowing perfectly well that you probably can't but also knowing that literature is indispensable to the world [which] changes according to the way you see it, and if you alter, even by a millimetre, the way a person or people look at reality, then you can change it. *James Baldwin*

In the catalogue *From Morality & Instruction to Beatrix Potter: An Exhibition of Books for Children* selected in 1949 from Edgar Osborne's collection, and reprinted in 1979 in a volume titled *A Token for Friends*, there is a section headed 'The School Story'. Eleven books are listed under the following note:

> The old style of school story has few devotees to-day. There is, however, still room for the children's school story provided writers who attempt such books are wide awake to modern trends in education and social development.

The first book mentioned is M. Pelham's *First Going to School, or, The story of Tom Brown and his sisters*, dated 1809. The fifth book is Thomas Hughes's *Tom Brown's Schooldays*, first published in 1857.

The seventh, published in 1891, is *The Cock-house at Fellsgarth* by Talbot Baines Reed. The last, published in 1899, is *Stalky & Co.* by Rudyard Kipling.

Though fifth in the list, *Tom Brown's Schooldays* is generally acknowledged as the progenitor of the boarding, or, as we English would call it, the public school story. Its author, Thomas Hughes, was born in 1822. It isn't fanciful, given the alternative title of Pelham's story, to suppose that Hughes read *First Going to School* as a child and that he remembered it when he named his famous hero Tom Brown. We can be sure that Talbot Baines Reed read Hughes's book (it is referred to in *The Master of the Shell*) and that he had it in mind when he wrote his own stories. We know that it was in irritated response to Reed's stories and his imitators, who were legion, that Kipling wrote *Stalky & Co.* In those few steps, from Pelham to Hughes to Reed to Kipling, we witness not only the birth and development into adulthood of the school story as a genre but also the emergence of the story of youth that is so often now called the young adult novel. In their effects on their readers we also witness the formative influence that the reading of fiction can have in people's lives, a significance I'll return to.

There is another, this time a personal step I'd like to take before moving on. It was during 1949, when the *Morality & Instruction* exhibition was showing at the Towner Art Gallery in Eastbourne on the south coast of England, that as a fourteen-year-old living in a town three hundred miles north of Eastbourne I first read *Tom Brown's Schooldays, The Cock-house at Fellsgarth* and *Stalky & Co.* A year later, after reading D.H. Lawrence's *Sons and Lovers*—a rather different story of youth, one much more like my own than the lives depicted by Hughes and Reed and Kipling—I decided that what I wanted to be, indeed what I *was*, was a writer of fiction. It took me another fifteen years to discover, as a result of working as a school teacher, that the kind of writer I am is an author of youth fiction. Though I don't write school stories, I do think of myself as working in the same tradition to which Hughes and Reed belong, and am proud of it.

So I am not, you see, a scholar, nor an academic researcher, nor a trained historian, but a fictionalist whose mind is attached to characters and plots and the language and forms of story. That's why I thought hard before accepting Margaret Maloney's invitation to give this lecture in memory of the scholarly librarian Helen E. Stubbs. I know the honour it confers and the standard set by previous speakers. Only when I realized that the centenary of Reed's death falls within days of this occasion did I decide to take up the challenge Margaret had set me. For so out of fashion are Reed's underrated books and so repudiated are some of his beliefs that I doubt he will be memorialized. Yet he deserves at least a nod of recognition. He is modestly important in the history of children's books, personifies a number of themes that run through writing for young people, is engaging as a character, and helps you ponder some of the mysteries that confront you if you are a practitioner, a maker or student of the literature whose history interests all of us who celebrate the treasure that is the Osborne and Lillian H. Smith Collections.

As befits an old-fashioned writer of old-fashioned stories, I want to begin in an old-fashioned way, by placing the man in his time.

Talbot Baines Reed was born, the third in a family of five boys, in the London borough of Hackney on 3 April 1852, and died forty-one years later on 28 November 1893. His father, Sir Charles Reed, also the third in a family of five boys, was a Member of Parliament, owner and manager of the Fann Street typefoundry, an ardent Christian of the dissenting Congregationalist persuasion, and a passionate supporter of church- as opposed to state-run education.

Reed attended the City of London school, a prestigious day, not a boarding establishment, which provided for the sons of the burgeoning middle-class London élite. He did well and remembered his time there with a deep affection that he invested in his school stories. As a boy, he was handsome, academically clever, good at Latin, Greek, French and German, musical, athletic, morally upright, unaffectedly religious, and sociable. In his mid teens he was awarded a Royal Humane Society medal for saving a cousin from drowning in rough seas off the coast of northern Ireland. Twice as a young adult he set off in the late afternoon and walked all night to cover the fifty miles from his home in London to St John's College, Cambridge, simply for the fun of having breakfast with an undergraduate cousin before spending the day visiting friends, watching cricket, and finishing up after midnight in his cousin's room enjoying student conversation. As you see, he was the very template of his own fictional heroes.

He did not attend the university. Instead, at seventeen, Reed joined the family firm, eventually taking over as Managing Director from his father. This remained his everyday full-time occupation till his early death, when the trade press recorded that he had been 'the practical element of the firm', a man notable for his 'courtesy and business tact'. Owing to his professional interest he began a systematic study of typefounding, out of which he wrote what is still the standard work, *A History of the Old English Letter Foundries*, a four-hundred-page illustrated volume of stylish scholarship first published in 1887, assiduously revised in 1952 by Alfred Forbes Johnson, then Deputy Keeper of the Printed Books Department of the British Museum, and reprinted as recently as 1974. Perhaps it was his experience of the problems of research while preparing this book that prompted Reed to be instrumental in setting up the Bibliographical Society during the last couple of years of his life. He was its honorary secretary and was to have given the fourth in the Society's first series of lectures, which he organized, intending to address the subject of 'The Relation of Typography to Bibliography'. It was never delivered. In January 1893 he fell ill with what his only biographer, Stanley Morison, says without explanation 'was in the nature of consumption'. He died the following November at his home in Hampstead Lane, Highgate.

Missing from this account is a whole other life, the one that mainly interests us here, and which in itself would have been enough to satisfy most people. Not only was he a full-time business man, a student of bibliography and the histories of typefounding and typography, an active member of his church, and an attentive family man, but he was also a prolific writer. For most of his adult life he was a regular reviewer for the newspaper, the *Leeds Mercury*, which was owned by his maternal grandfather.

And because of his involvement through his family with the Religious Tract Society, which founded *The Boy's Own Paper*, he became at the age of twenty-six a writer of school stories for boys. Thereafter, in fourteen years he produced a body of fiction which amounts to thirteen long novels, a collection of short stories, and numerous other stories, sketches and articles never published in book form.

Reed might have been describing himself when he wrote of a schoolboy character in *The Master of the Shell*:

Wake, of the Fifth, was one of those restless, vivacious spirits

> who, with no spare time on their hands, contrive to accomplish as much as any ordinary half-dozen people put together. He formed part of the much-despised band of fellows in his form contemptuously termed 'muggers'. In other words, he read hard, and took no part in the desultory amusements which consumed the odd moments of so many in the house. And yet he was an excellent cricketer and runner.

It is difficult to imagine how Reed fitted in everything he did, especially when we remember that he had no such aids as even a typewriter, never mind a word processor or fax machine, or motorcar. Towards the end of his life the telephone came in, and maybe that's the point. Stanley Morison suggests that Reed's final illness was caused by the new stresses that were troubling managers in the 1890s, a result of the increasing pace of business which—among other changes, like the railway system, cheap rapid mail, and the telegraph—the arrival of the telephone was helping bring about. As Morison points out:

> Middle-class men were beginning to suspect that they had driven themselves too far. Their doctors diagnosed a novel complaint, 'overwork'. [...] Reed's articles in the *Leeds Mercury* reflect these conditions of late Victorian life. More than one mention occurs of the 'high pressure' under which the middle classes (his term) worked.

But that was at the end. How did he manage to do so much before the modern strains of business overwhelmed him? Morison is good on that:

> The answer is threefold. First, Reed never worked against the grain. He realized that the conduct of the typefounding business involved 'workaday drudgery', but it was 'all in the day's work' in behalf of the art in which he believed. [. . .] Secondly, the answer to Reed's extraordinary productivity is implied in a paper entitled 'Odd Moments'. Here he ironically notes the contempt we feel for the man who works only from nine until seven 'and absolutely lets the rest of the day go by'. A loafer of this type is intolerable. He should at least read the newspaper

during lunch and bring out his tool-chest, microscope or book when he gets home. 'But', the writer proceeds,'odd moments are no more than spare moments; and it is a serious error to suppose that any number of odd and disconnected moments can ever equal a lesser number of even and consecutive moments. It is far more important to use the precious moments of our working day. All work worth the name involves, more or less, motion of the mind; and the mind, agile as it is, is not of that barrel-organ mechanism which can go on at a second's notice at the identical place or the identical time it left off an hour or so ago. Every hobby has to be kept in its place if it is not to assume a rivalry with our life's work. And though hard work, if the heart is in it, may be pure recreation, it is seldom that the quality of amateur work compares well with professional standards'.

These days I suppose we would say that what Reed possessed in abundance was self-confidence and commitment. He was also a true believer in personal and social virtues now considered obsolete. He spoke about these virtues in relation to his craft in a lecture to the Barnsley Typographical Association on 27 January 1891. Most of the men in the audience were jobbing printers. His preliminary remarks reveal a great deal about the man himself as well as his attitude to work. I want to quote a few of them for that reason and for one other.

Lately I've been asked to lecture to undergraduates who are majoring in literature and find they have little idea not only of why they are studying literature but of how and why the study of literature as an academic discipline, and the various theories of criticism, came about. In other words, they have no sense of history. Of course, it is the job of the old to be society's remembrancers, so I don't mind telling the story. But perhaps there is more to it than that. Perhaps over the last three decades or so we have lost an understanding of the importance of history, of knowing how we came to be as we are. Certainly the aberration called postmodernism encouraged this, for embedded in postmodernism is a dislike of tradition. It emphasized the ephemeral, the immediate, the short-term, image against substance, and therefore discounted any idea of permanence or connectedness. I think we are recovering from that now, though in a wobbly and sometimes ugly fashion, as, for instance, when the recovery is expressed in crude right-wing terms. Reed's words to the printers of Barnsley say something pertinent about all this. And if as you read what he said more than a century ago, you replace the words 'printing' and 'typography' with 'children's books' and 'writing for children' you will encounter something that is worth repeating now.

> Let me venture to preface my lecture tonight by reminding you that printing is above all and beyond all an art, and that the man who professes it must be an artist. The artist is not as other men. He must love his art. Still more must he love the beauty at which it aims. He must put something of himself into all his work—yes, if it be but a handbill or a newspaper column.
>
> The technical knowledge you are to get here, and, better still, the knowledge you are to give one another, will help to make you better workmen, and, I trust, advance your prospects in your calling. But it should do more than that. It should advance the calling itself. It should do something to raise the standard of what good printing ought to be, and encourage in you a discontent and contempt for what is vulgar, or tasteless, or ugly. We complain of the competition which injures our trade. The competition which injures most is the competition between the art and the craft in which it consists. One of the two must rule. If the art be not master of the craft, it must be its slave.
>
> By all means make what use you can of modern appliances, and machinery, and methods. But use them as artists: not simply for your own advantage, but for the glory of your art. That art, as you know, was not made yesterday. It comes down to us with old traditions and glorious prestige. I would commend to you, as an almost necessary part of the equipment of a good printer now-a-days, a study of the past. Read the history of printing. Examine the books of the old printers. See where they failed and where they triumphed. Try to get into touch with their spirit, and understand their methods. Take good note of the good that has survived, and equally good note of the false that has persisted. You will then, perhaps, realize better than you otherwise would do, what that art is of which you are today the heirs, and what is your duty towards those in whose hands

you are some day to leave it.

If the remarks I have to offer tonight aim to direct your attention to one aspect of this historical study of typography, it is because I am convinced that we cannot too often remind ourselves that in the school of the past, we may learn some, at least, of our most hopeful lessons for the school of the future.

The Beginning of *The Boy's Own Paper*

Just as today there are those who complain of the evil effects of video nasties on the behaviour of young people, so in mid-Victorian times judges and magistrates, schoolteachers and churchmen claimed that juvenile crime was stimulated by 'pernicious' blood-and-thunder trash that was the only reading easily and cheaply available to boys. What was needed, they argued, was an alternative, something morally wholesome yet entertaining. As no commercial publisher seemed willing to provide it, the Religious Tract Society decided in 1878 that their godly mission was to produce a weekly periodical to answer the urgent religious and social need.

Reed's family were closely involved with the Society. Talbot's grandfather, Dr Andrew Reed, religious Dissenter, Congregationalist minister, well-known hymn writer and worker on behalf of the insane and incurable, had as a child attended the inaugural meeting of the Society in 1799 and later wrote tracts for it. Talbot's elder brother Charles was one of the committee charged with setting up the new boys' magazine, which they decided must be as modern as possible in design, typography, illustration, choice of paper and printing. 'Its editors', claimed the prospectus, 'understand boyhood well, enter heartily into its pursuits and pleasures. True religion, in their view, is a spirit pervading all life, in work, in play; and in this conviction, rather than any purpose of direct doctrinal teaching, this tone is given to the Paper'.

However, this was not the first attempt at such an enterprise. Samuel Beeton had tried it with his *Boy's Own Magazine* as early as 1855, and others had set up in competition. Presumably none had succeeded sufficiently well to satisfy the Jeremiahs whose calls for worthy rivals to the pernicious dreadfuls stirred the RTS into action. Perhaps there is a parallel with the founding of Penguin Books in Britain in the 1930s. Penguins were not the first series of inexpensive paperback pocket-sized books, as some people now think, but they were the first to get it just right and to appear at just the right time. Like the RTS committee, Penguin also decided to use the best modern design, typography and printing methods. And like the members of the RTS committee, Penguin's founder, Allen Lane, believed that quality sells.

Beeton's magazine had been defunct for five years when the RTS decided to launch theirs. By then the word 'magazine' had become associated with monthly publication, and the RTS knew from the experience of their failed predecessors that the majority of boys wanted a weekly publication of a large enough format to allow for impressive illustration but not so large as to be awkward to hold. They knew as well that it had to be cheap. So, adapting Beeton's title, they called theirs *The Boy's Own Paper*, chose 21 x 30 cm format stitched into an orange-coloured cover and priced like the dreadfuls at one penny an issue. If preferred you could have it monthly with the weekly parts bound in a special wrapper that included a coloured frontispiece. Annually there was a Christmas gift-book version of the year's issues bound in cloth, stamped in richly decorative gold with an extra lithographed frontispiece in colour. The commercial astuteness of this plan is obvious. George Andrew Hutchison was appointed editor and remained so till his death in 1913, but Dr James Macauley, literary superintendent of the RTS, was brought in to work alongside him after Hutchison's first two attempts at the design of the magazine failed to please the Committee.

The first issue of *The Boy's Own Paper* appeared on Saturday 18 January 1879. The story on the opening page was titled 'My First Football Match', signed 'By an Old Boy'. The Old Boy was in fact the twenty-six-year-old Talbot Baines Reed. The Committee were not taking a chance on an untried writer, however, for this was not Reed's first attempt at writing for boys. Three years before he had published an article called 'Camping Out' in *Morning of Life*, a magazine for young people published by Thomas Nelson of Edinburgh. It described a boating trip on the Thames, an excursion he was later to recycle as a dramatic episode in his best-known novel, *The Fifth Form at St. Dominic's*, where it appears as chapter eighteen, 'A Holiday Adventure'. Besides that, he had for years contributed to and edited the family magazine, the *Earlsmead Chronicle*, a handmade periodical that gathered items from and was passed round the Reeds and their numerous relatives in London, Leeds and northern Ireland. Morison saw issues dating from May 1877 to December 1879, proving that Talbot was still busy producing it during the period when *The Boy's Own Paper* (hereinafter *BOP*) was started. All of which supports Morison's claim that Reed was from boyhood a keen amateur writer, was sure to be involved with his brother in the preliminary discussions about the new magazine, and that by inclination and experience he would be an ideal editorial assistant. Certainly, from the first issue to the time of his death fourteen years later he was one of the regular principal writers, quickly building up such an extraordinarily large following of readers that he became one of the most popular writers for young people of his day, not to say for some years after his death, as my own discovery of his books in my local public library in 1949 indicates.

So immediately successful was the *BOP* that the RTS started a sister magazine, *The Girl's Own Paper*, and from soon after its launch imitations were produced by commercial publishers in the hope of working the same magic. Of these *The Boys' World* was almost a straight copy in appearance, though, as is ever the way, its editor offered something more down-market and junky. 'I believe in giving you all kinds of light and easy readings,' he wrote to his readers, adding, lest the moral guardians accuse him of baseness, 'though, at the same time, I should blush to write anything of the "Penny Dreadful" type, or anything that a lad could not honestly show to his mother or sister'. (That prim claim reminds me of the hilarious moment during the trial for obscenity of *Lady Chatterley's Lover* in 1960 when counsel for the prosecution asked the jury whether they thought that *Lady Chatterley* was a book they would wish their wives or servants to read. I don't know if it is apocryphal that this same worthy lawyer, when asked how he decided whether or not a book was obscene, replied, 'I put my feet up on the desk and start reading. If I get an erection, we prosecute.' I wonder if the editor of *Boys' World* had some similar method of deciding what was and was not something a lad could honestly show his mother when, after all, most of the lads whose money he was after, and no doubt their mums and sisters too, were already regular readers of the sensational dreadfuls.)

A second keen rival to the *BOP* was *The Union Jack: Tales for British Boys*. Both papers poached some of *BOP*'s best writers, most notably G.A. Henty, who in 1880 became *Union Jack*'s editor. Naturally, the *BOP* editors did their best to warn their readers off its rivals and to maintain their lead by aiming 'to keep the *Boy's Own Paper* far ahead, in point of real merit, of any of its competitors, though we fear that all boys have not gumption enough to appreciate the vast difference between journals merely filled with improbable stories written to order by people who have never seen, and know little or nothing about what they profess to describe; and a paper like our own, in which both writers and artists occupy the highest place in public estimation, and are recognized authorities on the subjects with which they respectively deal'.

It worked. Only four years after starting, the *BOP* had built a circulation of 250,000 and went on to survive all its rivals, lasting until well after the Second World War before social and cultural changes brought it to an end: an extraordinary record and vindication of the RTS committee's judgement. In its time, millions of boys read it regularly and felt enormous affection for it for the rest of their lives. It was also influential, as it had set out to be. Which brings us to the subject of the school stories formulated by Talbot Baines Reed and why they were such soul shapers. Which in turn means it is time to meet the Doctor.

The Doctor of Rugby

He is both a real person and a fictional type. The real man was the Reverend Doctor Thomas Arnold, headmaster of Rugby School from August 1828 until his death on 12 June 1842, one day before his forty-seventh birthday. Arnold was regarded with such devoted affection by his pupils and became so renowned among his countrymen that even in my time in school during the 1940s and 50s he was held to be the very pattern of the ideal headteacher. But I doubt his fame would have spread quite so far or held up for so long without his hagiographic appearance in what must properly be accounted the first of the boys' school stories. Its author, Thomas Hughes, was a pupil at Rugby during Arnold's reign and adored him. His novel *Tom Brown's Schooldays* fictionally memorialized the Doctor with such persuasiveness that the character of the headmaster in almost all subsequent boys' boarding school stories was always called 'the doctor' and was some version—or inversion—of the real Doctor.

But the book did more than that. In its fictionally romanticized portrait of Rugby school, of the boys' behaviour, of the Doctor himself, and the emphasis it gave to the exciting dramatic moments of the story and certain aspects of the life of the school (sport, bullying, rebellious adventure) as against other less easily dramatized activities (academic study, the quieter cultural pursuits)—not just interpreting Arnold's views but misrepresenting them—Hughes put his own twist on Arnold's philosophy of what a good school should be and how it should be run. This account, rather than anything Arnold himself had said, done or written, from the time of *Tom Brown*'s first publication in 1857, formed the popular understanding of Arnold the man and his educational beliefs. Another example of fiction shaping people's view of reality. In this case it eventually proved fatal to the lives of a great many who were influenced by it, a point I'll return to.

Let's look for a moment at what Arnold—to my mind a great and attractive man—actually was like and what he did at Rugby; we'll be better placed then to consider his fictional reshaping. He did not come to Rugby unprepared. For eight years he had developed his ideas in a small school at Laleham on the Thames near Staines in Middlesex, not far from what is now London Heathrow. During that time his wife Mary bore seven of her nine children, the second of whom, imaginative, wilful, handsomely black-haired, blue-eyed, full-lipped Matthew, was to become a poet, critic and, as a government inspector of schools, even more influential in education than his father. Like his father's, his ideas have received their share of misinterpretation; when people speak of the morally improving value and function of reading great literature and of its place in education, it is of Matthew that they are talking. Happily, there are signs that he is regaining his proper reputation and attention after years of neglect.*

In her biography *The Arnolds* Meriol Trevor provides a succinct account of the changes Thomas Arnold made at Rugby. Before he arrived it was like many others of the so-called public schools of the day, places which originally were intended as free schools for the poorer classes but which by Arnold's time were not public at all, nor just any kind of boarding school, nor free, but exclusive, private, fee-paying establishments that primarily catered for the sons of the well-off and rich. Being English, they were (are) hierarchically categorized. By 1860 at the top of the pile were (are) the so-called 'Clarendon seven': Eton, Winchester, Westminster, Harrow, Rugby, Charterhouse and Shrewsbury. Later, two day schools were added to the premier league: St Paul's and Merchant Taylors'. Below them were second-rank establishments: King's Canterbury, St Peter's York, and E.M. Forster's school, Tonbridge, for example; and then lesser establishments below these. Which school you went to mattered more than how well you did there. Better to attend Eton and do badly than to perform brilliantly at some lower-ranking place. Thus was the English caste system bonded and entrenched. (Reed's newish day school, the City of London, would have been regarded with reluctant grace by the top public schools: a place for the dissenting and upstart middle class, it was nevertheless undeniably successful, academically and socially.)

There were one hundred pupils at Rugby when Arnold arrived. The previous head, Dr Wooll, had been an autocrat but seems to have allowed the boys to do pretty much what they liked in their spare time so long as they weren't caught. Meriol Trevor records that 'He had expelled boys for rape, but took no steps to protect them from each other [...] Some of the Sixth Form [sixteen- to nineteen-year-olds] spent as much as £100 a year on wine [a huge sum at the time]—now and again someone was expelled for drunkenness. Farmers complained of poaching and stealing but nothing was done to make the boys aware of the rights of others'.

* See, for example, *A Life of Matthew Arnold* by Nicholas Murray, Hodder & Stoughton, 1996; *A Gift Imprisoned: The Poetic Life of Matthew Arnold*, Ian Hamilton, Bloomsbury, 1998.

Trevor continues:

> There was at that time a good deal of talk about the evils of public schools, the antiquated forms of teaching, the lack of moral guidance and the consequent horrors of laissez-faire; as a result, the more responsible parents had their boys educated at home or at small schools like Arnold's own at Laleham [...] The trustees wanted Rugby improved so that numbers would increase and at first they were somewhat startled by Arnold's methods, especially his frequent use of expulsion.
>
> It was a considered policy. There were two types of boy whose presence he deplored and he invented two types of expulsion to deal with them. The hardened criminal who would only corrupt others was publicly expelled in disgrace. But the intellectually backward, physically overgrown boy, who had committed no serious offence, he would quietly 'superannuate', writing to the parents to explain that he thought it useless to keep the boy any longer at school, but suggesting methods of continuing his education. Some of these superannuated boys Arnold even invited to his home in the holidays, so he did not consider them in any sense disgraced. George Hughes, elder brother of the author of *Tom Brown's Schooldays*, was one of them.
>
> Arnold's methods were drastic but effective. The first thing he did was to get the trustees to increase the fees; with the proceeds he raised the salaries of the assistant masters and by 1829 was able to ask them, in consequence, to give up the curacies they held in the district and concentrate on teaching. He treated his masters as equals and had started at once a system of weekly staff councils, which was a complete innovation. From the beginning Arnold treated the school as a community and this was the secret of his success.

At first glance these changes look simply like a matter of imposing some intelligent discipline on an ill-disciplined institution. But they did more than that. By raising the fees Arnold ensured that parents not only took a closer interest in how their sons were behaving but thought twice about which of them to send to the school, tending to send only those who could benefit most from what the school offered. By seeing to it that his teachers were committed full-time to their work, Arnold aimed to improve teaching standards. In other words, what he wanted the school to offer was attention to learning, with an emphasis on academic success. That's why he quietly got rid of what Trevor calls the 'intellectually backward' boys; they were not going to add the kind of lustre he wanted to the school's reputation.

In fact, underlying his actions was a belief in the education of an élite, a body of highly educated men, disciplined, bonded in loyalty to each other as a special class of people, aware of their superiority, but conscious of the social responsibilities their position imposed upon them. Essentially, this was the ideal of the Guardians in Plato's hierarchy of Guardians, Warriors and Workers. Arnold so arranged the organization of the school that it modelled this philosophy, and ingrained it by daily living into the minds and souls of his pupils. Trevor tells us how

> Arnold made every member of the Sixth a praepositor [often now called prefects] but gave them duties as well as privileges and began the practice of inviting four to dinner each week. These were the youths who had been getting drunk the year before at great expense; Arnold treated them as responsible young gentlemen and most of them responded. Certainly the next batch did. And local inns were put out of bounds.
>
> Again, there had been an overflow of boys living in lodgings in the town. Arnold started the house system by asking the chaplain, Anstey, to take boys into his own new house. When Anstey retired in 1831, Arnold asked for the post, waiving the fee of £60 a year. The trustees not only gave it to him but insisted on his accepting the fee—which he used to improve the school library. He had not at first preached often but now he preached almost every Sunday at the afternoon service—short talks of from fifteen to twenty minutes, written on the same day, on topical subjects, [...] his voice was metallic and harsh, nor did he go in for oratorical eloquence; but he meant what he said and said it with passion. The boys were impressed; his words had a powerful effect.
>
> The same year, 1831, in an effort to make himself more available to others besides Sixth Formers, Arnold had an outside

stair constructed to his study and a pole put up, where he flew a flag when he was at home to any boy who cared to come. At first he had to invite them, but those who went spread the word that the new headmaster was not as stern as he looked and presently anyone felt free to call at such times. [...]

In the bad old days boys slept five or more to a bed and their fathers had to pay extra if they wanted single beds. Arnold insisted on separate beds for all boys without any charge. And no one, not even a master, not even himself, was to enter a boy's study without knocking. His principle was to trust boys and for the most part they responded. [...]

As for punishment, he disliked the old custom of flogging for everything. For most offences impositions were set and he introduced rules for what should merit a beating (administered by the praepositors) and ordained that normally no more than three strokes should be given; six was the maximum. As early as 1829 he told a friend that birchings had been reduced to only seven in the last half-year. [...]

Although in his famous list of educational aims Arnold put religious and moral principles first, gentlemanly conduct second, and intellectual ability only third, in practice he reformed this side of the school as much as the others. For generations at public schools Latin and Greek had been taught with little reference to history or modern literature; some Mathematics was thrown in as well. Arnold taught the classics in a live way, using ancient history to illuminate modern politics; he increased the Mathematics side and added French. He regarded French as very important and it was thus that he got modern history into the curriculum. History was Arnold's great interest.[...] 'Never read history without a map at your side,' was a maxim of his—and so geography found its way in too. In 1835 he succeeded in getting a Frenchman appointed to teach French, and German lessons were added, since the chief scholars of the day wrote in German.

Thus for a school in the eighteen-thirties the curriculum was thoroughly modernized; but Arnold did not expect a boy to excel in every subject. He instituted many prizes, even giving consolation prizes for effort, which he paid for out of his own pocket. If anyone won a university scholarship he would give a half holiday. Thus the prestige of intellectual work rose.

Remarkable how much of all this was still true over one hundred years later at the state day grammar school I attended between 1948 and 1953. The head was called 'the doctor'—or more usually just 'Doc' though never to his face. (I should add, he actually was a PhD, so the title was not undeserved.) The prefects, an élite bunch chosen from the seventeen- and eighteen-year-olds of the sixth form, ran the everyday life of the school, even to the extent of holding their own officially recognized court where boys could be tried for repeatedly committing serious offences, the worst punishment being a recommendation of expulsion to the headmaster. The court met once during my year as a prefect, an ugly occasion. Prefects had been allowed to beat until a few years before my time. Half-day holidays were given when boys won places at Oxford or Cambridge. Latin was still considered essential. French and German were taught as second languages. Close study of a canon of traditionally enshrined great literature was the core of the English curriculum. Teachers were required to wear academic gowns and were always addressed as 'sir'.

Two features missing from this description are perhaps the aspects of life in public schools that occupy most vividly the popular imagination: the official business of competitive sport, games, athletic prowess; and the system of 'fagging' that sustained the unofficial subculture of close friendships, crushes, covert sex, ragging (playing rough practical jokes), dares that led to risky adventures, millings (friendly rumpuses), serious violent fights, and bullying of all shades from teasing to torture.

You only need to glance at the chapter titles in *Tom Brown's Schooldays* to see where this popular image came from. Part One had nine chapters. The first three are about Tom's home. He doesn't arrive at Rugby till chapter four, which describes his journey there. The first chapter about his entrance into school life is titled 'Rugby and Football'. Chapter six, 'After the Match', describes in detail the traditional ritual initiation of new boys before the whole school in a trial by public mockery and depicts the heroic captain, Old Brooke, in action rallying the boys to the cause of the house and the school—'the best house of the best school in England!' Chapter eight, 'The War of Independence', introduces Flashman, the notorious bully, and includes the famous scene in which he tortures Tom by roasting the new boy's backside so badly over a fire that Tom 'turns deadly pale, and his head falls forward onto his breast'. Part One ends with 'A Chapter of Accidents': Tom poaches fish, is caught by the gamekeeper, and is flogged by the Doctor for his transgression. But this does not deter him from doing the same thing again many more times that season. Nor does it prevent him and his friend East from making the dangerous climb up a wall to the roof beside the school clock, an elevated hideaway they liked so much that 'they spent all their spare time there'. Finally, they inscribe their names on the minute hand, so disturbing the clock's mechanism that their miscreance is discovered. They are rewarded with a lecture from the Doctor and an imposition of thirty lines of Homer to learn by heart. Despite that, the very next day they deliberately do what they have been told not to do, visit a local fair, are found out and again flogged by the Doctor, who later threatens them with expulsion if they don't improve their behaviour when they return after the holidays.

Chapter seven, 'Settling to the Collar', in which a cross-country run severely tests Tom's courage, sounds a note that indicates from its very beginnings where the boys' school story is headed. This time it is the Doctor himself whom we see in action, giving one of those short sermons that were so famously inspiring. Hughes spends a lot of words analysing what it was that 'so seized and held these three hundred boys'. Here is the central passage:

> It was not the cold clear voice of one giving advice and warning from serene heights, to those who were struggling and sinning below, but the warm living voice of one who was fighting for us and by our sides, and calling on us to help him and ourselves and one another. And so, wearily and little by little, but surely and steadily on the whole, was brought home to the young boy, for the first time, the meaning of his life: that it was no fool's or sluggard's paradise into which he had wandered by chance, but a battle-field ordained from of old, where there are no spectators, but the youngest must take his side, and the stakes are life and death. And he who roused this consciousness in them, showed them at the same time, by every word he spoke in

the pulpit, and by his whole daily life, how that battle was to be fought; and stood there before them their fellow-soldier and the captain of their band. The true sort of captain for a boys' army, one who had no misgivings and gave no uncertain word of command, and, let who would yield or make truce, would fight the fight out (so every boy felt) to the last gasp and the last drop of blood.

What strikes me at once are the military metaphors: fellow-soldiers, captain, word-of-command, army, fighting, battle-field, yield, truce, the last gasp and the last drop of blood. I realize that Hughes intended this to be read as Christian spiritual language such as in popular hymns like 'Fight the good fight with all thy might', 'Soldiers of Christ arise and put your armour on', but two things bother me.

First, if the passage is intended to be a portrait of the real Doctor, as I have no doubt it is, it does not seem to me to be Arnold's way with words. In what I have read of him, he prefers metaphors drawn from the sacrament of the Last Supper, images of feeding, of serving one another, and the social virtues of God-focused community that the Eucharist encourages. 'Christians at their very social meal', he wrote in *Fragment on the Church*, 'could enter into the highest spiritual communion; it taught them that in all matters of life, even when separated from one another bodily, that same communion should be preserved inviolate; that in all things they were working for and with one another, with and to Christ and God'. Everything about him suggests the peacemaker not the firebrand, the builder not the destroyer, the sustaining father-figure not the bloodthirsty field-marshal. The military language and the cast of mind it betrays were not Arnold's, but the spin Hughes gave to his fictional Arnold.

The second thing that bothers me is that if a moral sermon couched in military language is inserted into the middle of a sequence of physically dramatic events—aggressively competitive games, brutally cruel bullying, and 'thoughtless and wilful' rule-breaking that ends up with the protagonist being flogged, and flogged not once in the first half-year of his time at the school but 'several times', by the very man who delivers the sermon—it is hardly likely that the spiritual will refine the secular but rather that the secular will corrupt the spiritual. The sermon's imagery and the story's drama work against the writer's intention that his fiction shall be morally improving and spiritually uplifting.

By the way, the detail about Tom's numerous floggings is interesting because it is another clue as to how far Hughes's fictionalized Rugby departed from the reality of Arnold's educational principles and his achievements. As Meriol Trevor records, Arnold greatly disliked flogging and by 1829 had reduced the total number of occasions in one half-year to seven. Yet Hughes has his fictional Doctor lamming into young Tom 'several times' in one half, not to mention the floggings he administers to other miscreants.

Hughes confesses in his preface to the sixth edition of his book that, like so many who write for children and youth, his 'sole object in writing was to preach to boys [...] in a shape in which it is most likely to get a hearing'. He hoped that if he was entertaining his message would take hold. And as usual when this is attempted by a less than first-rate writer, the entertainment took over the message and made it other than the preacher intended. Isabel Quigly sums up the effect of Hughes's novel in her book *The Heirs of Tom Brown*, the best study I know of the boys' school story:

> [...] Hughes's simple message went out, uninfluenced by Arnold's concern for things of the mind, or by his subtlety and originality. Even his political radicalism vanished into Hughes's spirit of pleasant, hearty democracy, in which the old squirearchy was to be allied with the rustic working class against the new industrialised city folk, proletarian or middle-class. Things went askew with Hughes's message, in more ways than one. He loved sport and believed in its good influence as a way of teaching courage, cooperation, and loyalty to a particular place, team, school-house or even country. What he did not foresee was that, because success in it demanded careful organisation and firm leadership, practice and professionalism, it would cease to be merely enjoyable and become a tyranny in the public schools. It would involve the tightening up of the time-table, the arrangement of the schoolboy's every free

> moment, the loss of every interest unconnected with it. The public schools in their heyday, particularly the 'hardest', most mainstream, had little time for hobbies, cultural interests, even wide reading, and certainly gave them little encouragement.

If Hughes can read that, he must be turning in his grave. If Arnold can read it, he must dying a hundred dreadful deaths. Arnold was a polymath, a thinker, a brilliant teacher, a lucid writer, affectionate, truly adult (a rare being), devout in a rational way that yet took his heart. Hughes had nowhere near the same stature. Another case of a great man unfortunate enough to be (mis)interpreted after his death, when he can do nothing about it, by a lesser man, and of the lesser man's message becoming the received orthodoxy. (The same misfortune has befallen his son Matthew at the hands of latter-day critical theorists.) Quigly quotes Oscar Browning:

> The most salient characteristic of modern public schools is the reception of games into the curriculum on an equality with work, if not into a superior position. Of this Arnold would have entirely disapproved. He would have seen that it ministered to a lower standard of effort, that it vulgarised intellectual labour, that it substituted self-indulgence for self-denial, and that it placed those boys in positions of command and influence who were frequently most unfit to exercise the one or the other.

And now that 'salient characteristic' has seeped from the English public school into the world at large and become the norm. Sportiness, competitive physicality, has been elevated into a new religion, the latest opium for the people, and infests politics. (And of course politicians; think of the embarrassing sight of American presidents in recent years, attired as modish athletes and panting round the streets of Washington, larding the lean earth as they wobble along, in an attempt to prove their toughness, their fitness, their competitiveness, while not one of them can write a sentence of any elegance or wit, nor open his mouth to speak without displaying the flatulence of his thoughts, the unfitness of his language, and the flabbiness of his intellectual muscle. Another instance of mismatch between image and the message it is intended to convey.)

Talbot Baines Reed was better than that, as a man and as a writer. He strikes me, in fact, as being very close to the ideal of an educated Englishman that Arnold hoped for. But as a day-school boy he had not had to endure the rigours of boarding-school life, which lack of experience allowed him to create a romanticized version of it in his fiction, while also he was a true believer in the character-building properties of competitive sport, which he therefore made a central theme in his novels. As a result he reinforced—entirely against his intention, in my estimation—Hughes's mistaken view of Arnold's educational principles. We must follow where that leads.

Reed and School

Stanley Morison tells us that by Reed's time

> the middle classes, especially the manufacturers and their counterparts in the City [of London], had money, brains and pride. Self-respect would not allow them to send their sons to the elementary schools, State or voluntary, established for the shopkeeping and lower classes. New schools, therefore, were founded for boys from the homes of well-to-do men of business. Thus, Radley came into existence in 1847, Clifton and Malvern in 1862. These, like the older schools, were dominated by the established religion, though a substantial number of the middle-class parents were dissenters from it. In 1867 a 'conscience clause' enabled boys who were not members of the established church to enter such schools [. . .]
>
> The average Victorian middle-class parent was earnest and far from being ashamed of it. The betterment of everything was an essential element in his make-up. Small wonder that, the more serious the parents, the more they desired their boys to read something which, while entertaining, was also accurately informative; above all, a book or paper that was written by men of education for boys who were also hoping to be men of education.

What these new schools did was assiduously ape the outward

and visible signs of the old 'Clarendon seven', their forms and customs, in order that they might appear equally sound and attractive to potential customers. They arranged themselves by the house system, in which as many as seventy boys of all ages (in Arnold's time from as young as ten up to nineteen, later on from thirteen) lived in a house ruled by a master but run by the older boys, the prefects, who had the privilege of fags: younger boys used as unpaid involuntary servants who did everything from making the prefect's breakfast and cleaning his shoes to running messages and accompanying him on walks. In other words, a form of slavery. The horrors, dangers and delights of fagging, the squabbles between older boys about them, between the fags themselves, and between fags and their owners are a feature of all public school stories as they were, by all accounts, a feature of everyday life in the real places. It is an amusing contingent irony that the term 'fag' in this usage is of obscure origin, not at all related to the same term used in the American sense of 'faggot', while the one thing everybody knows about fagging in English schools is that it provided a cover for illicit sexual friendships or abuse by an older boy of a younger. Arnold's insistence that every boy have his own bed had more to do with the boys' behaviour than their comfort.

The house system was also deliberately used to encourage competitiveness, and because it can involve everyone and has a drama that academic competitiveness lacks (having to do with closed rooms, sitting still, and hard intellectual work) this competitiveness was expressed mainly through sport. Playing for your house and supporting from the touchline or boundary if you weren't good enough for the team became a central requirement of everyday life, something on which a great deal of time and effort was spent. There was a hierarchy here too. Above the house teams and commanding a greater loyalty and effort still were the school teams. Playing for your school—better yet, being a team captain—was a pinnacle of boyhood success. Remember that the chapter in *Tom Brown's Schooldays* which introduces Tom to his new school is called 'Rugby and Football'. Right from the start the school story reinforced by fictionally glamorizing it the primacy and glory of playing the game, the battle to win and prove yourself a hero. In all of school literature no one is ever a greater hero than he who commands the school's best team and makes the winning score.

Living in cramped quarters run by older boys who had excessive powers of reward and punishment; spurred on by peers and teachers alike to obsessive physical effort and competitiveness in sporting activity; required to conform to a long catalogue of rituals, customs and manners with no meaning other than could be explained by an appeal to tradition; no privacy; such unappetizing food that it was necessarily supplemented by extras sent from home or bought from the school's tuck shop or, when opportunity allowed, from the local town; compulsory attendance at chapel every day; a regime that left little time to yourself: this was the daily life of a boy at public school in the 1870s when *The Boy's Own Paper*, that kind of reading the new middle-class parents wanted for their boys, was founded and Reed began writing for it.

That anyone could have liked such a life astonishes me, but clearly many did, or at least said they did when they remembered it with nostalgic affection in later life. What does not surprise me is that boys at boarding schools wanted to read fictions set in boarding schools. We all like to find our own life reflected in fiction's dramatizing mirror: the literature of recognition. Indeed, my belief is that, usually speaking, people only become committed readers of fiction when they have first discovered themselves in fictions, people of their kind, living their way of life and using their language. Especially so in adolescence, the principal time of the lived, as well as read, recognition story.

Equally, people like reading about the lives of those in enviable positions. So it wasn't just boarding-school boys who wanted public school stories, but also a much larger audience of the less advantaged and well-off, 'ordinary' children who after 1870 attended by requirement of law the newly established state and church-managed neighbourhood schools. In other words, my claim is that through the fictions about them the public school ethos was spread into the community at large, as much as it was by the teachers and managers of the new state day schools, which aped the public schools in whatever ways they could. What the fictional fee-paying public-meaning-private boarding schools depicted, teachers and pupils attempted to recreate in their real free state-provided day schools.

All the state secondary schools I attended or worked in during my years as a pupil and a teacher in the 1940s, '50s and '60s divided pupils into houses, for example, even though they were day schools and there were no actual houses where the pupils lived. All of them made a much greater fuss of competitive games and of the teams and their captains than they made of academic achievement. Cups and plaques were prominently displayed. All had a prefect system with its accompanying privileges, duties and powers (and usual abuses of all three), though there were no fags. Most had some kind of tuck shop where pupils could buy the kind of unhealthy food adolescents crave. All set great store by rituals such as speech day or founder's day when prizes were handed out and a notable figure gave an address that was expected to conclude with an amusingly expressed appeal to the head teacher for a half-day's holiday as a reward for the school's obvious success. In most the teachers wore academic gowns, and in the couple where they didn't the head wore one for the assembly (required by law) that began each day with a hymn, a prayer, a reading from the Christian bible, an address by the head or a visitor, and a reading out of organizational messages. During the religious segment Jews, Roman Catholics and any whose parents held strong other-than-Protestant-Christian beliefs, withdrew for their own separate devotions, returning for the secular bits, a public demonstration of difference not without significance in a ritual mainly intended as a bonding celebration of conformity and togetherness. All of us belong, but some of us belong more than others.

There are plenty of schools in Britain and the ex-British colonial countries, where the colonizers embedded in their educational systems the English public-school ethos, that are entirely like that even now. I have visited a number of them in Australia, for example. We are not talking here about a finished history.

All of which is introductory to saying that when rival magazines appeared and the editors of the *BOP* were thinking of how they could keep ahead of the field, the inclusion of a serial set in a fictional public school was the answer they hit upon and Reed was the man they chose to write it. His one-off pieces—adventurous episodes such as 'My First Football Match' and 'A Boating

Adventure at Parkhurst', as well as portraits of 'boys we have known' such as 'the sneak', 'the sulk', 'the boy who was never wrong'—had built him a readership and prepared him for the long haul of a serialized novel-length story including the kind of episode and typical characters that would make it popular.

His first essay in the form was not, however, quite the finished design. *The Adventures of a Three Guinea Watch* recounts the progress of a fob watch from school to college, then from England to India, where as a possession of an officer in Her Majesty's army it takes part in the troubles at Lucknow. From home and school and dear old England to the army that made and kept the Empire, a story told by the watch's final owner to his children is an account of daddy's life and exploits. Reed's very first story for the magazine celebrated victory on the football field, his very first serial celebrated the heroic career of a player in the national game of empire building. The best man, the best team, the best school, the best nation, naturally of course, wins. That is only just and the way life should be.

I'm not at all sure why Reed used the device of the watch and took in the whole of a life's story. Perhaps he hadn't yet quite understood the potentials of a narrative set only in a school. But according to Morison, his editor knew exactly what was wanted:

> [. . .] a writer capable of creating an individual who was a hero; to place him in a social setting in which he could face risks and be seen acting in a Christian, manly, courageous and considerate fashion towards his fellows. The obvious frame for such a relationship between writer and reader was to set a personality in the kind of young collectivity known as a 'public school'.

What we are observing here is the birth of a genre. *Tom Brown's Schooldays* had appeared on the scene almost like an act of special creation, without any antecedents. At the time it really was, as Charles Kingsley told his publisher, Daniel Macmillan, 'the only one of its kind' (though some might suggest a forerunner in Thomas Day's *Sandford & Merton* begun in 1783 and finished in 1789). But Hughes thought of his story as an autobiographical fiction, not as an out-and-out novel. He wrote it because his son was about to go off to Rugby and, thinking over what he'd like to say to him on such an important occasion, 'I took to writing a story, as the easiest way of bringing out what I wanted'. His 'whole object' was 'to get a chance of preaching'. Hughes was not thinking of form, not of an artwork, a made object, but of a message, which is why *Tom Brown* is more a collection of episodes loosely linked by the central character than a structured novel exploiting the resources of a particular genre.

So instant was its success that it wasn't the only book of its kind for long. Books are conceived in many ways, but one of the most frequent results from a reader's desire either to emulate or to better a book he has loved or disliked. My guess is that dissatisfaction with Hughes' book provoked F.W. Farrar, then a teacher at Harrow, to write *Eric, or Little by Little*, published only a year after *Tom*. Again, 'The Story of "Eric",' Farrar revealed, 'was written with but one single object—the vivid inculcation of inward purity and moral purpose', and again like Hughes, Farrar based his story on his own schooldays at King William's College on the Isle of Man. Hugh Kingsmill was probably right when he described *Eric* as 'perhaps the most luxuriant example of emotionalism over the young', 'the sort of book Arnold might have written had he taken to drink'. Even so, I find myself agreeing with Jenny Pausacker that 'the main impression left by the book is of passionate sincerity rather than sentimentality'. Certainly *Eric* touched a nerve; for a long time it was hugely popular.

Talbot Baines Reed could not abide it, however, and, as Morison reports, regarded *Eric* as

> a religious tract thinly disguised as a school story. According to Reed, the dean administered a 'powder' compounded of religious dogma and Christian morality, rendered palatable, as he hoped, by the narrative 'jam' of school life. Unfortunately, the dean knew so little about youth that his boys are lay figures and his book failed for that reason. Reed's opinion of *Eric* appears in more than one of his articles in the *Leeds Mercury* [...] Reed was convinced that the powder element was too aggressive, the jam insipid, and the whole compound nauseous for any boy.

Here is a real novelist at work, pondering—to express it in

traditional rather than post-structuralist terms—the nature of form, the veracity of character, the relationship of theme to character and plot. Behind all of which stands tone: the relationship of author-narrator (the author's 'second self', to use Dowden's term of 1877) to implied reader. What Reed could abide least of all was the preacher's voice, the sanctimonious declaration, delivered from an authorizing pulpit raised six feet above contradiction, of homilies that used anecdotes for no other reason than to prove the preacher's superior wisdom.

We know from his reviews in the *Leeds Mercury* that Reed admired R.L. Stevenson, thinking *Doctor Jekyll and Mr Hyde* 'a masterly shocker', and that he was a fan of *Treasure Island*, published in book form in 1883 but before that as a magazine serial, an ideal model for someone setting out as a writer of serial fiction for boys. At the same time he regarded Henry James, whose *Portrait of a Lady* was published in 1881, as among the best contemporary novelists. Anyone who genuinely held that opinion in those days, when James was an avant-garde taste, unquestionably possessed an astute literary mind.

This, then, is my main argument. Talbot Baines Reed, a man who loved people, was sociable, energetic, intellectually and physically almost hyperactive. A voracious reader and a prolific enthusiastic writer, he thought carefully about the nature and purpose of fiction and studied its techniques and form. There was much he wanted to say, all of it based on a philosophy we would now characterize as Christian humanism. He understood boys and, to judge by his fiction, liked them, and was on their side in the sense of regarding them as one of 'us', not one of 'them', though his instinct was rather that of friendly adult than buddy. He knew that the best way to teach boys was through stories that depicted as truthfully as he could manage the actuality of their lives.

More than a teacher, however, he was a storyteller. He used to say that literature was a luxury but fiction was a necessity. And this made him a natural serial-writing novelist rather than a preacher or school teacher. After reading Hughes or Farrar one feels it is the lessons that matter; after reading Reed one feels it is the story that matters above all. The result is much greater and longer-lasting satisfaction, and far greater attention to the *mean-*

ing that his stories create within themselves than to the message their author tried to impose upon them. In this sense Hughes and Farrar are moralizing journalists who used stories, whereas Reed is an artist who made novels. Hughes and Farrar, whatever their qualities, are the kind of writers who give children's books a bad name; Reed, whatever his failings, is the kind of author who creates fictions of childhood and youth that enrich the literature of our language.

Now it is time to celebrate those qualities, without ignoring the failings, of Reed's books, fictions that speak to us still as writers and readers of the literature of adolescence. And as all acts of criticism, all reviews, all discussion of literature, whether scholarly or academic or informal gossip between friends, are essentially autobiographical, I'd like to begin where I began myself, with the book of Reed's that first attracted my attention.

The Truth about Rollitt

The Cock-house at Fellsgarth. Perhaps it was the robust raunchy air of the title that took my fancy. I was fourteen; the resonating innuendo of 'Cock-house' appealed to an emergent adolescent in late 1940s Britain, when everything interesting about sex was kept secret. Of course, I knew the intended meaning was the champion house in a school, mainly at sports. I understood this from *Tom Brown's Schooldays*, a favourite book at the time. And the name Fellsgarth has the air of a north Yorkshire dale, like Aysgarth in the countryside near where I lived and where I took myself for brooding solitary walks. I was drawn at that age to the solipsistic pleasures of moody Wordsworthian romanticism but of course longed for dramatic release. So I suppose I assumed that the book would provide some youthful excitement set in my own territory. Whatever caused me to take the book off the library shelf, it was one of the characters who caught my imagination and whom I remembered ever afterwards. Indeed, in my memory the book was all about him, he was the central character, it was his story.

I did not reread the novel between that youthful encounter and preparing this appreciation. Imagine my surprise—to use that hallowed phrase from novelists of earlier days—when I discovered that it was not until chapter six and page sixty-eight that the character I remembered with such affection even entered the book and that he was not the central character at all. At first I felt aggrieved on his behalf, and a little annoyed that my memory was so faulty. Of course, I reminded myself that in my original reading I had taken from the book what I wanted and ignored the rest, recycling Reed's narrative into a story that clothed my own image.

That is what readers always do, for we modern readers know that every story, indeed literature as a whole, is, as Paul Ricoeur puts it, 'a laboratory for thought experiments that, thanks to the mediation of reading, we may apply to ourselves'.

The character who located me in Reed's novel is called Rollitt, a head-butt of a name that suits his bulky physique and awkward personality. Reed was always good at names. This is how he handles my fictional companion's entrance into the story:

> Rollitt of Wakefield's [house] was a standing mystery at Fellsgarth. Though he had been three years at the school, and worked his way up from the junior form to one of the first six, no one knew him. He had no friends, and did not want any. He rarely spoke when not obliged to do so; and when he did, he said either what was unexpected or disagreeable. He scarcely ever played in matches, but when he did he played tremendously. Although a Classic, he was addicted to scientific research and long country walks. His study was a spectacle for untidiness and grime. He abjured his privilege of having a fag. No one dared to take liberties with him, for he had an arm like an oak branch, and a back as broad as the door.
>
> All sorts of queer stories were afloat about him. It was generally whispered that his father was a common workman, and that the son was being kept at school by charity. Any reference to his poverty was the one way of exciting Rollitt. But it was too risky an amusement to be popular.
>
> His absence of mind, however, was his great enemy at school. Of him the story was current that once in the Fourth, when summoned to the front to call over the register, he called his own name among the rest, and receiving no reply, looked to his place, and seeing the desk vacant, marked Rollitt down as

> absent. Another time, having gone to his room after morning school to change into his flannels for cricket, he had gone to bed by mistake, and slept soundly till call-bell next morning. 'Have you heard Rollitt's last?' came to be the common way of prefacing any unlikely story at Fellsgarth; and what with fact and fiction, the hero had come to be quite a mythical celebrity at Fellsgarth.
>
> His thrift was another of his characteristics. He had never been seen to spend a penny, unless it was to save twopence [...] The only extravagance he had ever been known to commit was some months ago, when he bought a book of trout-flies, which rumour said must have cost him as much as an ordinary Classic's pocket-money for a whole term.

When I tell you that as a youth I was a shy and dedicated loner, that when I read *Cock-house* I had newly started as a late entrant at an academic grammar school where most of the boys' fathers were middle-class professionals such as lawyers and doctors whereas mine was 'a common workman', that I loathed games and played them as rarely as possible (once being threatened with expulsion for ducking out of the twice-weekly torture but sometimes fantasizing about one day walking on to the sports field and dazzling the crowd with a show of brilliance at cricket or rugby), that being boringly self-conscious and tidy by nature and squeaky clean from motherly attention I found absent-mindedness, untidiness and grime sentimentally enticing (I tried for a while to cultivate all three but with depressingly unimpressive results), when I confess all this, you will see that Rollitt was an anti-hero to my liking.

For the rest of the book he comes and goes as the plot requires, which eventually solves the mystery of his father, who is indeed 'a common workman', and of who pays to keep him at an expensive school—two well-off unmarried women. Meanwhile, he almost drowns, is saved by a younger boy who thereafter he befriends and protects with brusque affection, is accused of a crime, is exonerated, plays superbly in a vital football match, the boys against men, and finally decides at the end of the book 'to the general regret, but to his own satisfaction' to leave Fellsgarth 'for the more congenial course of a school of engineering', an unheard-of, indeed revolutionary decision for a public school hero in Reed's day. It took my breath away even in 1948. I remember being so thrilled I cheered out loud. It seemed to me the most heroic act in the entire book, a demonstration of courageous individuality, of total independence from conformity and convention. Rollitt had broken free. Truly an anti-hero of the kind I aspired to be, though the term was unknown to me then. And I thought that was what the story was about, what it was intended *to mean*.

That is still 'my' *Cock-house at Fellsgarth*, even though, since my recent rereading of the book, I can acknowledge that Jenny Pausacker's account, the analysis of a trained and sophisticated critic, is also right about the novel's unintended ideology. Pausacker is an Australian writer of fiction and a student of modern critical philosophies and techniques. As her argument is careful and her study—a doctoral dissertation—has not been published I'd like to quote from it at length; her approach, by plot summary, shows just how much my naive, youthful reading didn't notice, so involved was I with Rollitt alone:

> In *The Cock-house at Fellsgarth* the conflict is between Moderns and Classics, who compete for control of the school institutions. Rivalry accelerates until Dangle and Clapperton, the head of the Moderns, leave the football team, taking the rest of the Moderns with them. Yorke, the Classics captain, striving for peace, closes down the school clubs, which puts the Moderns in disfavour. The Modern juniors withdraw their support, and so gradually do the rest of the house. Finally, when Yorke proffers friendship to Clapperton in a Christian spirit, Clapperton is glad to accept.
>
> The central conflicts in these books [*The Fifth Form at St. Dominic's, The Willoughby Captains, The Cock-house at Fellsgarth*] accelerate in their dimensions, from a conflict between individuals, to a conflict between two possible heads of the school, to a conflict between two halves of the school. Each conflict highlights a different aspect of school life. Oliver Greenfield [in *The Fifth Form at St. Dominic's*] seems to be acting contrary to the code of honour, but turns out to have been acting very honourably. Willoughby [the school of *The*

Willoughby Captains] seems to have to choose between brains and brawn for its captain, but Riddell [the chosen and brainy but unathletic captain] develops sporting abilities. In both cases the resolution is proof of the infinite flexibility of the school system. [And, one might add, the flexibility of the boarding school as an enclosed world, paradigm of the outside world, run mostly by the young characters themselves, where almost anything required of a story can happen.]

The conflict in *The Cock-house at Fellsgarth* is more complex. The rivalry between Classics and Moderns has no relationship to the content of the subjects being studied, but concerns their relative prestige. The issue, however, is a foregone conclusion from the point where we learn that among the Moderns are a number of boys 'who boasted in public of their wealth with a freedom which was particularly aggravating to the Classics scholars, who were for the most part boys to whose parents money was an important consideration', and Yorke has 'the guidance and help of a Divine Friend', while Clapperton is 'a big smirking fellow, rather loudly dressed...' Reed continues Hughes's identification of the public schools with the gentry, and begins the condemnation of the nouveau riche which was to be carried on in the formula school story. [...]

With the character of Rollitt, Reed's only working-class schoolboy, the situation is definitely out of control. Unjustly suspected of theft, Rollitt is the misunderstood character of *The Cock-house at Fellsgarth*, as Greenfield is of *The Fifth Form at St. Dominic's* and Wyndham of *The Willoughby Captains*. Rollitt is a combination of acceptable and unacceptable traits—amazingly strong and undeniably talented, but untidy, sharp-tongued and withdrawn. Rollitt's working-class origins are the explanation of his non-conformity [which] cannot be given a place in the school world and [he] is eventually dismissed to engineering school. If the wealth of the Moderns cannot be tolerated, neither can Rollitt's poverty.

Reed's main concern, it emerges, is to endorse the status quo.

Or, as Wyndham, the heroic ex-captain of Willoughby School puts it at the end of the novel that is, to my mind, the most interesting of Reed's books, 'Willoughby first, your house next, and yourself last.' Which beyond the school gates translates to: country first, school (or family) next, yourself last. Certainly, that was Reed's manifesto throughout his life. But it is wrong, I think, to suggest that this is the overriding idea in his stories. To a significant degree Pausacker's accusation could itself be accused of presentism: she judges Reed by today's attitudes as if he could have been as aware of them as she is. That is all right so long as we do not at the same time condemn Reed for something he could not know about, and so long as we do not claim that this is all there is to say about him. I wonder what people will be making of Jenny Pausacker's novels and of mine in a hundred years' time, if indeed they still seem worth reading and talking about then? What ideological errors will we be accused of that at present we are entirely unaware of committing? Everyone belongs to their time. It is the fate of all writers to become dated, but some possess qualities that keep them alive, making it possible to set aside their period prejudices and blindnesses. In the best, Shakespeare, for example, Jane Austen, George Eliot, D.H. Lawrence, their datedness is the least part of their writing and so they seem in many respects as pertinent and enjoyable now as they ever were.

I'm not claiming such transcendence for Reed. But I am suggesting that within the school-story genre he is the outstanding figure, the one who uses the form seriously to make a canny study of human behaviour. In fact, I'd say he is alone in this. He is the only boarding/public school story writer who produced a body of work which shows development of his ideas, of his handling of narrative and character, and whose use of language—witty, fluent, clean of weary cliché, accurate in dialogue, well orchestrated—is worth attention for its own sake. (*Stalky & Co.* matches up, but Kipling wrote only this one school-story book, not a body of work devoted to the genre.)

Ideological constraints framework everything written for children today as in the past. The dominant message, now as in Reed's day, is that one must learn to behave oneself well in whatever way is currently defined as 'well'—in other words, one must know one's place as a human being and not rock the boat more than that little which makes life and stories entertaining. Apart from this framing message, Reed's novels can be read—and in my view were intended—as dramatically entertaining meditations on aspects of everyday life that are in philosophical and moral terms difficult to contemplate. Read like this, *The Cock-house at Fellsgarth* is a meditation on moral and physical bravery and courage. *The Willoughby Captains* deals with the nature of leadership, government and politics. It includes, for example: appointment by royal decree (the head master, who rules by 'divine right' of the unseen school governors, appoints without consultation or election the head boy and the prefects); a (mock) parliament that functions precisely like the British parliament at Westminster; adversarial debate conducted as in the House of Commons; deputations to the king (boys to the head master); committees, ad hoc and appointed, and the way they work; and so on. *The Master of the Shell*—in which the main protagonist is a young teacher, whose life we see from his point of view and out of sight of the schoolboys, a viewpoint exceptional in its own time and still sufficiently unusual to be 'modern' in its attitude to what the novel for young readers can do—is an investigation into what it means to be a good teacher, what authority means and how to handle it well, what (in)justice is and how it works.

Very few children's and youth novels today can equal that for thematic range and the unoppressive seriousness with which Reed approaches his readers. He expects them to match him in language and content, and assumes they want to know about the adult world—that they want to become adult, not remain adolescent.

Pausacker demonstrates convincingly how Reed confirms the status quo, but there is another side to him which his stories press home much more forcefully. In each of his books a central character, usually *the* central character, has to find the courage to stand on his own until the rightness of his actions can be proved or revealed. In Reed's fictional world, it may be necessary to know your place in the ordering of society, but within that claim on you, you must be ready to stand up for your convictions and what you know to be right, even if that means you stand alone against your peers, are ostracized, and derided. Within your social conformity you must be prepared not to conform, if conforming means living an untruth simply to remain accepted and acceptable. Naturally, this requires moral, intellectual and physical courage. And far more than messages about maintaining the status quo, that is what all of Reed's books are about, what they *mean*.

Which is why I find myself disagreeing with Pausacker's reading of Rollitt's departure from Fellsgarth. Reed is careful to suggest that it was Rollitt's own choice: we are told he left 'to the general regret' and 'to his own satisfaction'. He has proved his innocence, his loyalty to his house and school, his moral and physical bravery, his academic cleverness, and even by the end has gained great popularity. The easy satisfaction both to Rollitt and to the reader would have been to keep him at the school, a model of honour. This would have confirmed the status quo because the message would have been that the system plays fair by those who, like Rollitt, it adopts as well as those born into it, that justice eventually wins the right for the right, and we could all have felt that glow of satisfaction which comes from such condescension by the haves to those who have not and who are allowed to move up in the social system.

It was more morally courageous of both Rollitt and his creator to reject Fellsgarth in favour of the socially less attractive school of engineering. To do this wasn't preserving the status quo but rather was to suggest that the public school is not the be-all and end-all, that for some talents there may be better kinds of education than places like Fellsgarth can provide. Precisely because it was against reader-expectation and, perhaps, -approval to send Rollitt to such an unfashionable alternative institution, we know a point is being made. Perhaps we should remember that Reed himself chose not to take the usually preferred route for men of his class and go to university, as had his eldest brother and his cousins, but to go straight from school into what was essentially an engineering business, typefounding. In a sense, he had made the same choice as he gives to Rollitt. So, in the delicious way that narratives can carry parallel contradictory meanings, it is right of Pausacker to conclude that Reed *unwittingly* favoured the status quo, and equally right to claim, as I do, that he *wittingly* wrote about resisting the status quo and even acting against it, should that be necessary. A mark of Reed's stature, his above-the-ordinariness, is that his novels subvert his own ideological stance.

Deconstruction has emphasized that there is a self-destructive defect in every work of art as in everything created. What is the weakness at the heart of Reed's stories? We'll find it by looking for a pattern repeated in book after book that, like the opaque patch on x-ray film, betrays the fatal flaw.

In Reed's stories there is always a hierarchy, determined not by Reed but by the structure of English public schools of the time. At the peak an élite group of older boys, the prefects, are themselves led by the élite of the élite, the school and house captains and their henchmen. Below them a middle group of boys are lords in waiting, the restive young bloods who harry or support the current leadership. Then, lowliest of all, a third group, the carefree first- and second-year youngsters, are foot soldiers who provide the tale with its broad humour, its pranks and light relief (the equivalent of the rude mechanicals in Shakespeare). From their ranks the prefects choose their fags. Reed sometimes characterizes them as naive rascally little animals—Tadpoles and Guinea-pigs, for example, in *The Fifth Form at St. Dominic's.*

By Reed's time, the English public school had become not simply a place of élite education, on Dr Arnold's model, but an institution designed to produce imperial bureaucrats whose training equipped them for the work of running the Empire, including of course the homeland of Britain itself. In order to do that reliably (which means turning out people who could be trusted to do nothing that would undermine what was in fact a fragile, notional authority based on the work of very few men), the chosen boys had to be moulded into 'one of us' within the closed system of the school, which itself modelled the world beyond the school gates. If you showed yourself unreliable during this training period, or in some way unsuitable (as both Pausacker and I suggest that Rollitt is unsuitable), you were persuaded to leave or were thrown out. In this twisted version of Arnold's vision, to be a Guardian you must give yourself wholeheartedly to the system, support it unreservedly and live according to its customs, rituals and mores, through thick and thin, no matter what. What was *not* wanted, therefore, was intellectual doubt and inquiry because that would have led to dangerous questioning of the system.

Hence the denigration of intellectual activity and the cultural Philistinism that is still a feature of British life. In France, for example, to call someone an intellectual is a compliment; in Britain it is always an insult.

In Reed's stories this creed is worked out in roughly the same way each time. One of the élite or would-be élite, the hero of the story, finds himself somehow in the wrong—accused of theft, or of being inadequate to his position, or having cheated. He either cannot or more usually will not justify himself. Without complaint and with courage and determination he carries on doing his duty in the way the system dictates he must, studying, running his house, whatever—even if his own closest friends desert him and he stands alone. During this time he displays physical as well as moral courage. Then by some plot device, and at the expense of an unworthy character whom the hero overcomes and who is later removed from the school, his rectitude is proved. The fickle plebeian mob of juniors swings back to his support, and by dint of some dramatic event, usually a vital sports match, the hero saves the entire school from disgrace and is accorded all but godlike status.

In other words, the in-training élite try by suffering and rejection one of their own (a member of the élite), who, by enduring with courage both moral and physical, proves himself not only worthy of overall authority, of kingship, but by his personal sacrifice and godly gifts, saves the honour and reasserts the power of the whole body of the select. One version of this is the Christ story. Another is Superman. It is also the story of fascism: the super race from whom emerges by trial and courage the superman under whose divinely conferred gifts the super race rules the world. That is the flaw in the public school story, the same flaw that lies at the heart of so many of our hero legends, the difference being that the school story was a real story, which the fictional version merely dramatized for popular consumption by those who belonged to the élite and by those over whom they ruled. Which is why it is correct to say, as Correlli Barnett puts it in *The Collapse of British Power*, 'Except for young Nazis or Communists, no class of leaders in modern times has been so subjected to prolonged moulding of character, personality and outlook as British public school boys'.

The public school story, which, as Isabel Quigly and Jenny Pausacker among others have pointed out, was formulated and shaped more by Talbot Baines Reed than by any other writer, played a key part in communicating the formative images by which British boys were moulded, modelling for them the ideals, the attitudes, the customs and rituals held to be essential.

I said earlier that Reed was a true believer and suggested that this might be his Achilles heel. Like all true believers he was completely convinced of the rightness of the way of life he lived every day himself and depicted in his stories. But because his personal qualities are so attractive his beliefs seem attractive too. He once wrote of the printer and bibliographer William Blades, the man who, after his father, had the greatest influence on him as a young man, that he possessed 'an unaffected goodness'.

The same tribute could be paid to Reed himself. Everything we know about him suggests a man of the most straightforward and modest goodness. 'Ainger [...] was popular', he wrote of a character in *The Master of the Shell*, 'because he had won the mile, and was upright, and meant what he said, and said what he meant. No boy of whom the same can be said could help being popular'. That was Reed himself. 'Riddell was no coward', he wrote of the hero of *The Willoughby Captains*, 'nor was he one of those sickly individuals who, not satisfied to be struck on one cheek only, invite a repetition of the assault on the other side [...] he had sufficient British instinct to move him to stand up for himself'. Reed again, this time unapologetically revising the Gospel on which he based his beliefs to fit the Guardians' view of human nature and revealing his triumphalist chauvinism without a hint of a blush because he believed it to be right, indeed obvious, that the divinely ordained destiny of the British ruling class was to rule the world.

The Battle of Waterloo, said the Duke of Wellington (at least according to Montalembert), was won on the playing fields of Eton. One hundred years later, thousands of young Englishmen, products of the state as well as the public schools, enthusiastically gave themselves to death on the battlefields of Flanders in the belief that they were doing their heroic duty: country first, school second, self last. They had acquired that belief, that view of their fate, as much from their reading of school stories as from anywhere else. Which is why I spoke earlier of fiction shaping people's view of reality and, in the case of the genre that began with *Tom Brown's Schooldays*, eventually proving fatal to the lives of a great many who were influenced by it. It does not seem surprising to me, therefore, that after the disaster of the First World War, when it was no longer possible to take seriously the nineteenth-century public school ethos and the inevitability of its superiority, the boy's public- and boarding-school story declined into superficial pastime comedy. Had he still been alive—and he easily could have been—what would Reed have made of this appalling outcome, and what would he then have written? But he died before the whistles blew and the Guardians went over the top, determined never to turn the other cheek and always to behave as a true Englishman should.

Fictions in Form

What is there left to celebrate? In general, of course, the loss of that idiotic conviction. And the freedom ambiguous doubt, intelligently used, can give. More specifically: the 'unaffected goodness' of Reed's life, and his formulating place in the history of writing for young readers. To most people, his work is now of antique interest only; I doubt that reprints would succeed with a large enough readership to justify their cost, though I have to say that as I was rereading him recently I was constantly struck by the thought that his stories could be adapted into very attractive television dramas. However, for those of us with a particular interest in the art he practised, his narrative qualities are worth attention.

From the historical point of view, for example, his books are full of details that tell a lot about how mid-Victorians treated their young, how they ran their less-than-top-notch schools (Reed's fictional schools, whatever their claims, are not exactly Eton and Harrow but more the kind of establishment that ape them). Here, for instance, is Reed's description of what a school 'house' was like at that time. Mark Railsford, the young first-job house master and protagonist of *The Master of the Shell*, is shown round his territory, on the first morning of term and before the boys have arrived, by the head master, Dr Ponsford, inevitably referred to simply as 'the doctor':

After breakfast Mark was conducted in state to his house. The floors were all damp and the carpets up; beds and wash-stands were piled up in the passages, and nowhere was a fire to be seen.

'There are your rooms,' said the doctor, pointing out a suite of three apartments opening one into the other, at the present time reeking of soft-soap and absolutely destitute of furniture. 'You will find them comfortable and central. The inner room is the bedroom, the middle your private sitting-room, and this larger one the house-parlour. Now we will go to the dormitories and studies. You understand your head boys—those in the Sixth and Fifth— have a study to themselves; the Shell have studies in pairs, and the junior school work in the common room. But all these points you will make yourself familiar with very shortly. As a house master, you will of course be responsible for everything that takes place in the house—the morals, work and play of the boys are under your supervision. You have four Sixth Form boys in the house, who are prefects under you, and in certain matters exercise an authority of their own without appeal to you. But you quite understand that you must watch that this is not abused. The house dame [usually called the matron], Mrs. Farthing, superintends everything connected with the boys' wardrobes, but is under your direction in other matters. I shall introduce you to her as we go down.

'I refer you to the school time-table for particulars as to rising, chapel, preparation [usually called homework by day-school boys], and lights out, and so forth. Discipline on all these points is essential. Cases of difficulty may be referred to a session of the other masters, or in extreme cases to me; but please remember I do not invite consultation in matters of detail. A house master may use the cane in special cases [that is, administer corporal punishment by beating the offender either on the hand or the backside with a whippy stick of bamboo], which must be reported through the masters' session to me. So much for your house duties.

'As Master of the Shell, you preside at morning school there every day, and, as you know, have to teach classics, English, and divinity. In the afternoon the boys are taken by the French, mathematical, and chemical masters. But you are nominally responsible for the whole, and any case of insubordination or idleness during afternoon school will be reported to you by the master in charge, and you must deal with it as though you had been in charge at the time.'

But for the absence of history and geography in the subjects mentioned, this is almost exactly what life at Rugby under Dr Arnold must have been like for teachers and boys. Note, for example, the absence of any reference to sport, which had no part in the curriculum and was organized by the boys themselves. Note also the spartan and somewhat rough-and-ready nature of the accommodation, the layering of discipline from head master via house masters and teachers to prefects, each with his absolute powers, though, when you examine it carefully, in practice those with the most immediate and considerable power, direct in effect on the happiness or otherwise of the boys' everyday lives, were the prefects. But Reed was a novelist, not a historian. Passages like this are not there simply to inform us; they always have plot significance.

One of Reed's strongest qualities is his pacing of narrative. Because his stories appeared first as serials, his plots possess that sequencing of character and action which is designed to keep people reading from one chapter to the next. And because he was writing for a known audience of boys ranging from about ten years of age to early adulthood, he includes younger and older characters and a variety of types so carefully judged that everyone has a fictional character to empathize with.

For the same reason, he developed a style that uses the clear, taut, often short sentence, quite unlike the verbose and tautological writing of many of his later imitators. He often speaks directly to the reader, sometimes teasingly, at others wittily drawing moral conclusions from the behaviour of his characters: 'He is not the only boy who gets his head turned now and then by the unexpected discovery that he is virtuous. Is he, reader?'; 'peril and achievement bind friends together, as no mortar binds bricks'; 'he had learned the secret that sympathy is the golden key to a boy's heart'.

Unlike most of the formulaic school-story writers who followed him, Reed can transcend the limits and contrivances of plot, turning his long stories into true novels, books that investigate for the sake of it the nature of life, regardless of 'entertainment value' or the trite demands made by readers of pastime fiction. (One of the most interesting of these passages is in chapter nineteen of *The Master of the Shell* where the young house master spends a night looking after a deliriously ill boy. The scene is necessary because it is only while he is delirious that the boy can reveal the culprits of the crime that is the 'engine' of the story. But Reed's handling of the scene is far more extensive and detailed than is required by the plot. He makes of it a full and moving, as well as medically accurate, description of a death-threatening illness, Victorian style, and of the moral and spiritual experience of nursing the sick. It is the 'stuff' of life that is being examined. The scene gives one hint among many of the fine literary novelist for adults Reed could have become had he wished.)

One could go on for some time, evidencing besides all I've mentioned so far the satisfying range of Reed's humour, the veracity of his dialogue and the skill with which he uses it to advance the story and reveal character, and the smoothness of his plotting (with a few notably awkward moments), but space won't allow. Best, perhaps, and appropriate to end by celebrating this novelist I've come to admire, learn from and enjoy by allowing his words to speak for themselves, especially as his books are now difficult to get hold of. I've chosen a scene from what was Reed's most popular book, though it isn't my own favourite, *The Fifth Form at St. Dominic's*. In it one of the junior boys, Stephen Greenfield, confronts the prefect Loman, for whom he fags. The fags have decided to go on strike, an unheard-of defiance against the older boys, and now Stephen must face the consequences. It's a scene that demonstrates how skilfully Reed conveys plot and character through the cut-and-thrust of dialogue as well as by the perspicacity of the narrative commentary, how he builds tension, and the pleasing pace of it. I'm also impressed by how effectively he narrates the violent action—clear, trim, never sensationally offensive, yet properly upsetting nevertheless. And I'm interested in the attitude of the teacher, Mr Rastle, a good man at heart, to what has happened, and how he deals with the incident—one of those documentary passages I mentioned earlier that tell us how things were then between adults and children.

Indeed, if all the rebels had been like Stephen, the fags at St. Dominic's would be on strike to this day. He contemplated martyrdom with the utmost equanimity, and the Inquisition itself never saw a more determined victim.

The morning after the famous 'cricket feast' gave him his first opportunity of sacrificing himself for the good of his country. Loman met him in the passage after first class.

'Why didn't you turn up and get my breakfast, you idle young vagabond?' inquired the Sixth Form boy, half good-humouredly, and little guessing what was in the wind.

'I'm not idle,' said Stephen.

'Then what you do mean by not doing your work?'

'It's not my work.'

Loman opened his eyes in amazement, and stared at this bold young hero as if he had dropped from the clouds.

'What!' he cried; 'what do you say?'

'It's not my work,' repeated Stephen, blushing, but very determined.

'Look here, young fellow,' said Loman, when he was sure that he had really heard correctly, 'don't you play any of your little games with me, or you'll be sorry for it.'

Stephen said nothing, and waited with a tremor for what was to follow.

Loman was hardly a bully naturally. It was always easier for him to be civil than to be angry, especially with small boys, but this cool defiance on the part of his fag was too much for any one's civility, and Loman began to be angry.

'What do you mean by it?' he said, catching the boy by the arm.

Stephen wrenched away his arm and stood dogged and silent.

Nothing could have irritated Loman more. To be defied and resisted by a youngster like this was an experience quite new to him.

'Just come to my room,' said he, gripping his fag angrily by the shoulder. 'We'll see who's master of us two!'

Stephen was forced to submit, and allowed himself to be dragged to the study.

'Now!' said Loman shutting the door.

'Now!' said Stephen, as boldly as he could, and wondering

what on earth was to be become of him.

'Are you going to do what you're told, or not?' demanded Loman.

'Not what *you* tell me,' replied Stephen, promptly, but not exactly cheerfully.

'Oh!' said Loman, his face becoming crimson, 'you're quite sure?'

'Yes,' said Stephen.

'Then take that!' said Loman.

It was a sharp box on the ears, suddenly administered. Stephen recoiled a moment, but only a moment. He had expected something a good deal worse. If that was all, he would brave it out yet.

'Don't you hit me!' he said, defiantly.

Loman could not stand to be defied. His vanity was his weak point, and nothing offended his vanity so much as to find any one as determined as himself.

He took up a ruler, and in his passion flung it at the luckless Stephen's head. It struck him hard on the cheek. The blood flushed to the boy's face as he stood a moment half stunned and smarting with the pain, confronting his adversary. Then he rushed blindly in and flung himself upon the bully.

Of course it was no match. The small boy was at the mercy of the big one. The latter was indeed taken aback for a moment at the fury of his young assailant, impotent as it was, but that was all. He might have defended himself with a single hand; he might have carried the boy under one arm out into the passage. But the evil spirit had been roused within him, and that spirit knew no mercy. He struck out and fought his little foeman as if he had been one of his own size and strength. For every wild, feeble blow Stephen aimed, Loman aimed a hard and straight blow back. If Stephen wavered, Loman followed in as he would in a professional boxing match, and when at last the small boy gave up, exhausted, bleeding, and scarcely able to stand, his foe administered a parting blow, which, if he had struck no other, would have stamped him as a coward for ever.

'Now!' exclaimed Loman, looking down on his victim, 'will you do what you're told now, eh?'

It was a critical moment for poor Stephen. After all, was the 'strike' worth all this hardship? A single word would have saved him; whereas if he again defied his enemy, it was all up with him.

He did waver a moment; and lucky for him he did. For just then the door opened, and Simon entered. Stephen saw his chance. Slipping to the open door, he mustered up energy enough to cry as loud as he could,

'No, I won't;' and with that made good his escape into the passage, as done up as a small boy well could be without being quite floored.

[... T]hat afternoon, Stephen with his face all on one side, his eye a bright green and yellow, and his under lip about twice its ordinary thickness, took his accustomed place in the arithmetic class of the Fourth Junior.

'Why, Greenfield,' exclaimed Mr. Rastle, when in due time the young hero's turn came to stand up and answer a question, 'what have you been doing to yourself?'

'Nothing, sir,' remarked Stephen, mildly.

'How did you come by that black eye?' asked the master.

'Fighting, sir,' said Stephen, rather pompously.

'Ah! what did you say forty-eight sixths was equal to?'

This was Mr. Rastle's way. He very rarely hauled a boy over the coals before the whole class.

But after the lesson he beckoned Stephen into his study.

'I'm afraid you got the worst of that fight,' he said.

Stephen, who by this time knew Mr. Rastle too well to be afraid of him, and too well, also, not to be quite frank with him, answered meekly,

'The fellow was bigger than me.'

'I should guess that by the state of your face. Now, I don't want to know what the fight was about, although I dare say you'd like to tell me [Stephen was boiling to tell him]. You small boys have such peculiar reasons for fighting, you know, no one can understand them.'

'But this was because—'

'Hush! Didn't I tell you I won't hear what it was about, sir!' said Mr. Rastle, sharply. 'Did you shake hands afterwards?'

'No, I didn't, *and I won't!*' exclaimed Stephen, forgetting, in his indignation, to whom he was speaking.

'Then,' said Mr. Rastle, quietly, 'write me out one hundred lines of Caesar, Greenfield; and when you have recollected how to behave yourself, we will talk more about this. You can go.'

[... Stephen] was groaning over his imposition late that evening in the class-room, feeling in dreadful dumps, and wishing he had never come to St. Dominic's, when a hand laid on his shoulder made him start. He looked up and saw Mr Rastle.

'Greenfield,' said the master, kindly, 'how much of your imposition have you done?'

'Seventy lines, sir.'

'Hum! That will do this time. You had better get to bed.'

'Oh, sir!' exclaimed Stephen, moved far more by Mr Rastle's kind tone than by his letting him off thirty lines of Caesar, 'I'm so sorry I was rude to you.'

'Well, I was sorry, too; so we'll say no more about that. Why, what a crack you must have got on your cheek!'

'Yes, sir; that was the ruler did that.'

'The ruler! Then it wasn't a fair fight? Now don't begin telling me all about it. I dare say you were very heroic, and stood up against terrible odds. But you've a very black eye and a very sore cheek now, so you had better get to bed as fast as you can.'

And certainly the pale, bruised, upturned face of the boy did not look very bright at that moment.

Stephen Greenfield went off to bed that night in a perturbed state of mind and body.

Needless to say, such a hero as Stephen not only survives but lives, gloriously to captain his school cricket team, by which time he has become 'an object of special awe among the youngsters of the Fourth Junior, who positively quake in their shoes whenever his manly form appears in the upper corridor'.

It is an unintended irony that at the beginning of the scene Reed should teasingly compare Stephen's skirmish with 'sacrificing himself for the good of his country', for we can calculate that by 1914 he would have been about thirty-nine years old, just the age of the senior regimental officers who commanded teams of another kind, which were sent out to fight and die for England with all the stubborn determination Stephen had shown against

Loman. Country first, school next, self last.

Talbot Baines Reed knew the power of story to shape and shift us. What finally I learn from his life and his fiction is that we must be self-consciously careful of the ambiguity of what we write, for the young above all, and riddlingly thoughtful of everything we read.

Pick up a Penguin

You could count the books in our house on one hand. A do-it-yourself medical manual, necessary to keep the doctor's bills at bay; a stubby ugly small-print dictionary for use on the rare occasions when formal letters had to be written; a fat one-volume encyclopaedia, which I think must have been a give-away from a newspaper in the competition for readers during the 1930s; and a volume of Aesop's fables in a comfortably impressive format with thick good-quality paper and wonderful colour plates of illustrations. My mother would tell me the stories while I stared at the pictures. The Aesop was my first loved book.

Every Christmas, from about the age of six in 1941, I was given three Bumper Annuals, those large-sized volumes of rough, almost cardboard-thick paper littered with black and white line drawings, some of which you were intended to colour in or finish off. I coloured them all with waxy crayons, whether you were meant to or not. That was all I did, because I couldn't read properly until I was nine. I could read individual words, but the trick of making the words into sentences and the sentences into paragraphs evaded me. Until one evening just after my ninth birthday when I was looking at the pictures in a book I'd been made to bring home from school, and suddenly everything came together and I heard voices talking in my head. One voice was telling the story, the other voices were the people in the story talking to each other. I was almost frightened for a moment, certainly shocked, as well one might be when a bookful of strangers suddenly inhabit your head all unannounced. I still remember the moment vividly, with as much excitement, as fresh, as immediate as ever. My parents were in the room at the time; my mother noticed that a change had come over me and realized what it meant. 'What's he doing up at this time?' I remember my father saying, and my mother's reply: 'Shut up, you fool, can't you see what he's doing!' What I was doing must have been a relief; worry about my backwardness had meant gloomy meetings at school. Even so, I still didn't become a frequent reader.

Scarlet fever brought that about ten months later. I came down with it on my tenth birthday, 27 December 1944. In those days a reportable disease, you were sent to an isolation hospital for three weeks. When I arrived home after my incarceration a welcome-back present from my paternal grandmother, the only educated reader in the family, was waiting for me, a copy of the Puffin edition of *Worzel Gummidge* by Barbara Euphan Todd, illustrated by Elizabeth Alldridge. I did not understand then, and did not know till many years later, that this had been the very first of the Puffin Story Books published in December 1941, nor did I have an inkling of the importance of Puffin as a publishing phenomenon, and no premonition of the place its parent, Penguin Books, would quite soon occupy in my education and development. With the insouciance of childhood, stimulated by the pleasure of being back home and sitting in coddled convalescence beside the comforting familiarity of our living-room fire on a cold and rainy January day, I simply did what came naturally: I looked at the pictures, being careful to do so in the right order, from front cover, page by page, to back. (I don't know where this came from, but I have always felt it somewhat scandalous, a mistreatment of a book, or at least letting the author down, if one doesn't first of all look at the pages in the bound order.)

One picture occupied my attention more than any of the others: the full-page drawing of Susan sitting in the farmhouse kitchen eating with a large spoon from a pudding bowl. The wartime hospital food had been meagre, dull and repetitive (one of the first things I told my mother when they let me out was that I never wanted to eat rice pudding again—we'd had it once a day and sometimes twice) so I was curious about what Susan was eating. And why out of a pudding bowl, something my mother would have thought 'not right'? The only time I was allowed anything out of a pudding bowl was when I scraped the leavings from the chocolate filling my mother made for my favourite sponge cakes, and I didn't do that with a large spoon but with my finger.

In the end there was only one way to find out. Read the story. So I set to and the result was that for the first time I read a book from cover to cover without wanting to stop, and for the first time the words in print flowed so fluently that I didn't even notice them but was aware only of the theatre in my head playing out the story as it happened, it there in me, me there in it. A kind of paradise, a life fuller, livelier, richer than my own everyday life, and one replete with meaning.

But it was a life that did not remain closed between the covers of the book. As soon as I reached the scene depicted in the drawing of Susan and the pudding bowl, and discovered that she was eating bread-and-milk, which she was given to keep her from catching cold after getting soaked during a walk across the fields when she and her brother found Worzel Gummidge, I stopped reading long enough to explain to my mother that I just had to have something called bread-and-milk, that I had to have it now, and that I had to eat it with a large spoon out of a pudding bowl. I don't recall any questioning of this demand; probably my mother was happy to indulge any odd whim on the day her only child was returned to her. I do recall insisting that the spoon be a serving spoon because no other looked big enough when compared with the one in the picture.

Because of this, *Worzel Gummidge* became not only the first book I read from cover to cover not wanting to stop (or the story ever to end), it was also the first book I read while eating. As I didn't finish it that day (I was a slow, hearing word-by-word reader then, and still am), it also became the first book I read to myself while in bed, and the first for which I made myself wake up early so as to go on reading in the morning. Also the first book I reread, start to finish for its own sake, which I did the instant I reached the end the first time. For no reason I can explain, I kept count of the number of times. Thirteen during the next two years.

Four months after my first reading of *Worzel Gummidge* we moved to another town. Across the road from our house lived a boy of my own age with whom, because of proximity rather than for any more companionable reason, I made friends (or rather, as I was chronically shy, more true to say he made friends with me). Alan was a reader. I wouldn't say a passionate or particularly thoughtful reader, but a reader in the way of people brought up to it by parents who like a good story to pass the time when they aren't doing anything better, which they are of course most of the time, so what they usually call 'reading for pleasure' is for bedtimes, and for slack times at weekends, and on holidays. And in the way of people brought up to it, Alan assumed I read as he did and, in the casual way of such people, gave me the book he had most recently read so that I could read it too. The book was *Just William* by Richmal Crompton. I read it, though with less imperative feelings than those that drove me back and back to *Worzel Gummidge*, and afterwards Alan and I giggled at William Brown's adventures and read bits to each other that then seemed more inordinately hilarious than they had done when we read them to ourselves. This was my introduction to the added pleasure of sharing enjoyment by talking about what one has read.

The rest of William Brown and a shelf-ful of Biggles came to me by the same route along with a catalogue of other, mostly now forgotten titles. I wish I'd kept a list, something I didn't think of doing until the Great Penguin Moment that comes later. Very soon, when to his utter amazement he found I not only did not belong to the town's public library but did not even know such an institution existed, Alan made it a condition of our friendship that I join. The place scared me to death. Had Alan not been with me, twisting my arm and blackmailing me, I'd never have gone inside. It seemed very large and dauntingly mysterious, sepulchrally hushed, and anyway, how did you get past the woman behind the high magisterial counter, and when you had, how the hell did you know what to look for among all those tank-traps of bookcases full of spine-out books? Well, Alan showed me how the feat was accomplished, though only after parental signing of an application form for membership. ('What'd they want to know all this for?' Dad asked, suspicious of local government forms. 'And, by God, it talks about fines on the back. Just you watch yourself, you hear!')

Quite certainly, without Alan and the public library, I'd have got no further than *Worzel Gummidge*. What going to the library with Alan every week did was establish a routine. Because we went, I always borrowed something. (I rather felt that if I didn't I'd be told off by the librarian.) Because Alan wanted to swap books so that we both read the same ones and could talk about them, I also read what he borrowed. This went on week after week for two years.

Selecting what to read happened this way. We'd go to the

library. As soon as we were inside, we'd separate so as not to be tempted to talk and get told off. You were allowed to borrow two books at a time. Usually, we each had at least one book in mind: another William book, say, or whatever was a current fad. But we each had to find something new as well. And because we separated I had to find what I wanted by myself. In those days, library books were usually covered in heavy-duty library bindings, the bookish equivalent of army combat dress: robust, made to last, and camouflaged in black, dull dark blues and greens and browns so as to blend into the landscape. Titles and authors were paraded on the spines in uniform type and no distinguishing marks to denote rank or regiment. You're on your own, soldier.

In the children's rooms things weren't always quite that spartan. But there were no dust wrappers, nor anything much on the covers to suggest what was inside, except sometimes a one-colour dye-stamped decoration or drawing; nothing as image-fixated as these days. And nothing like a blurb to tell you something about the story or a publisher's gratuitous statement of superlative praise. All you had to go on was the title, author, and the pages of the book itself. Yet it was during this time I managed to find for the first time *Treasure Island*, Ransome's *Coot Club* and *The Big Six* (on the strength of which my father and I taught ourselves to sail during a Ransome-inspired holiday on the Norfolk Broads), *Tom Brown's Schooldays*, Talbot Baines Reed's *The Cock-house at Fellsgarth*, *Stalky & Co.*, *Alice's Adventures in Wonderland*, *Masterman Ready*, *Prester John*, and a long-time favourite read once a year till I was into my twenties, *The Wind in the Willows* (but not Beatrix Potter, Enid Blyton, Edith Nesbit, *The Secret Garden*, or many another childhood usual, which remain a deeply regretted absence from my imagination).

At that time, between my eleventh and fourteenth birthdays, I was fascinated by nature and harboured a romantic idea of eventually going to sea in the wake of some of my great-grandparently relatives. So at first I'd look for stories to do with the countryside or ships. Radio was a help with this. I used to listen to a regular programme on BBC *Children's Hour* called *Wandering with Nomad*. This was a precursor of the TV nature programmes by the likes of David Attenborough, who probably listened to *Nomad* as well, I'd guess, he's the type in aspic. And

Nomad had a precursor too. He was called Romany. These were Boy-Scouty uncle figures who rambled the countryside with a dog and a young (male) friend, representative of the listener, during which they encountered flora and fauna and told you about them.

Both Romany (the Reverend G. Bramwell Evens) and Nomad (Norman Ellison) wrote books, factionalized adventures based on their radio programmes. Nomad's were beautifully illustrated with woodcuts by Tunnicliffe. Somehow or other, probably when browsing the library shelves, I discovered them. Under their influence I rambled the river Tees and Swaledale in North Yorkshire, earnestly keeping notes of everything I saw and then writing them up in a Nature Diary afterwards in the manner prescribed by Nomad in one of his programmes. This was the first writing-of-my-own I did. To be quite sure I got it right, I wrote to Nomad asking for more advice. He replied within a week, his answer closely handwritten on the back of a picture postcard of scenes from his rambles. This was the only time I ever wrote a fan letter, and now that I know just what size of postbag he must have received every week and what a labour it can be to reply to fans, I'm full of admiration for Ellison's care and dedication to his reader/listeners.

My new-found interest in books meant that Christmas-and-birthday presents (the contiguity of the dates combined the two) now included books-by-request. William, Biggles and Nomad came to me that way and were the start of my personal library. Identification books, too, for use during my nature trips. And the comic-strip weeklies, *Beano* and *Dandy*, both of which Alan introduced me to as well. An only child, shy and solitary by temperament, and never happy in the town I'd been brought to, for me reading was, I suppose, an expected occupation. But during the patch of time I'm describing, I never thought of it like that. It was simply something I did in the way I went to the cinema twice a week and to the music hall and theatre once a week, and listened to radio. I knew I enjoyed it but it was no more special than anything else. Probably, if asked, I'd have said the cinema was what I liked best; certainly I felt most comfortable there—imaginatively at ease, and never feeling it was hard work, which reading often was, even when the book was gripping and 'readable'.

The change from general to particular happened because of a school and a school teacher and a particular book during a couple of years between my fourteenth and sixteenth birthdays. Before I come to this, however, so as to avoid misunderstanding, I'd better relate that other people had already played a part. The change wouldn't have happened without them. One of my infant school teachers, Miss Ainsley, read aloud to us every day and made us act out the stories she read. I've never forgotten her for that. A primary school teacher in the town we moved to when I was ten read aloud to us every afternoon. I particularly remember her reading *Heidi* by Johanna Spyri. Because I failed the eleven-plus examination, my first secondary school was a secondary modern. There, an English teacher, Freddy Foxon, read aloud to us often and gave us play-reading lessons regularly, which I enjoyed very much. He read poetry to us as well, and encouraged us to keep a scrapbook of potted biographies of writers. It was all contingent preparation for Darlington's Queen Elizabeth Grammar School, Jim Osborn, and my discovery of Penguins.

When I was thirteen and a half, in 1948, it was decided I should be moved to the town grammar school as a late entrant. Not me alone, but about fifteen other late developers from the town's secondary moderns. This was a result of the 1944 Education Act and Darlington Education Committee's determination to match opportunity and ability as best it could. Jim Osborn was the astringent, witty, briskly critical, uncompromising head of English. For him, literary reading was the heart of education. At first I was taught by other members of his staff, with only the occasional mind-storming lesson with him. Nevertheless his personality pervaded the place. You didn't have to be taught by him to be influenced by him.

My first formal encounter involved Kubla Khan. Jim strode into the room (he never strolled, sauntered or even walked anywhere, but did everything with a sense of urgency), carrying a record player. This he plugged in, switched on, put a record on the turntable, looked at us with his cross eyes through bottom-of-bottle glasses, said 'Listen', and dropped the needle onto the record. What emerged sounded to us mesmerized pupils like gobbledegook. After four seconds, he lifted the needle, pointed to the nearest boy and said 'Repeat what you heard'. The boy couldn't. Jim went round the class. No one could. 'Listen,' he said again, now with dreadening emphasis. Four seconds of gobbledegook again. Another tour of the class. Nothing. Tension starched the air. This time eight seconds. But no one could manage even a syllable of the sound. One boy burst into tears. It was all too much. Jim gave out a set of books. A page number was rapped out. 'Listen, again.' What we were listening to was:

In Xanadu did Kubla Khan
A stately pleasure-dome decree . . .

Jim read the poem to us himself. Made one or two of us have a go at the first lines. Played some more of it on the gramophone. Asked us what we thought of it, if we liked anything about it, whether we knew anything about the author. Gave us the story in his own words. Made us listen to the way the sounds were orchestrated. No concessions. No pandering. No attempt to ingratiate. An insistence on precision. Sweated work. And an assumption that we would discover in this something enjoyable and worth possessing.

I don't know about anyone else in the room that day, but I do know that when Jim swept out, gramophone hanging from one hand, books clutched to his chest in the other, the black drape of his academic gown (compulsory wear for staff in those days) flying behind him, the world for me had changed. Words had come to mean more than something. Language was a sacred river. Poetry was fertile ground. No book was ever the same again, never simply a means to a pastime activity that filled spare corners of my life.

The following year Jim took us for half our English timetable: his friend and deputy, Richard Fairbairn, a compassionate, affectionate, likeable man who first brought Shakespeare to life for me, took the other half. Between them, they made reading English literature the best thing one could do.

I should add here that, throughout my school years, from the time Alan took me there, I was borrowing every week from the public as well as, later, from the Grammar School library. The list of authors I came across includes not only those writers for young people already mentioned but also, when I was made to move into the adult room, Balzac, Eden Phillpotts, Chekhov, Pamela Frankau, J.B. Priestley, Dostoevsky, Graham Greene, Turgenev and a great many more indiscriminately chosen by nosing them out from the regimented ranks and sampling their pages every now and then till the moment came when they seemed to be just what I needed. Usually, I'd mention I'd read them to Jim, who would put his own gloss on the selection (a consultation that once produced the memorable reply, 'J.B. Priestley is not the sort of writer you have time to read'). I mention this because I want to acknowledge the importance that the free public library system had for me. If Alan had not made me join the library, would I ever have become a regular reader? Had I not become a regular reader would I have progressed enough at school to be transferred to the Grammar? Had I not been sent to the Grammar...? People made all the difference in my life, but none of them could have done it without the books made available to me free by the school and public libraries—a provision chosen by the expertise of the librarians, whose belief at the time was that they must select what they considered to be the best that had been and was currently being published. Their equivalent in commercial publishing was Allen Lane and Penguin Books.

What started me buying books I can't remember. Because Jim said we should, I think. All I know is that by the time I was fifteen I was receiving five shillings (25p) a week pocket money from my father. Half of this was spent on my twice-weekly visits to the cinema (necessarily supplemented by secretly bunged subsidies from my mother). The other two-and-sixpence was spent, without fail, on a book.

There was a ritual to the book buying. During lunchtime a couple of times a week, say Tuesday and Thursday, I walked the ten minutes from school to Dressers the booksellers on High Row where I browsed the Penguin shelves. At that time, a paperback cost between one shilling and sixpence and two-and-sixpence. All the fiction was in the famous orange-banded covers, crime in green, non-fiction Pelicans in light blue, biography in dark blue, and so on. I never saw any Puffins, which must have been kept somewhere else in the shop. It seems strange to me now that my passion for *Worzel Gummidge* did not reach the knowledge that it was a Puffin Book, that there might be more like it, and that I should have a look. I take this as evidence of innate stupidity and a failure of curiosity.

Unlike the hardbacks, the paperbacks were stacked spine out, never presented face up. So one had to look along the shelves (two stacks of about eight to ten shelves, as I recall, nothing like the plethora there is now) and go by title and author. After a while, I knew the back stock so well I could quickly pick out the new additions and would examine them to see if I wanted them. Any of the others that provoked interest that day were also looked at more closely. Of course, mostly there were no cover pictures, certainly never anything sensational or eye-grabbing. I remember being upset when Penguin started making a feature of pictorial covers and got rid of the broad orange bands with the title in sans serif black-on-white between, thinking it a disgusting development, cheapening the list into the sort that Pan Books and Corgi were.

Not much cover come-on, and not much by way of blurbs either. On the back was a small black-and-white photo of the author along with a brief biographical note that always left me wanting much much more. The only picture I now remember is Evelyn Waugh in his army officer's cap, staring rather sternly at me from the back of what must have been *Brideshead Revisited* or *Decline and Fall*. I see that on the 1948 edition of *Vile Bodies* he is in civvy shirt, tie and jacket and in left profile, hair slicked back in thirties' brilliantine style, and the biographical note takes up two thirds of the back cover, so I don't know where I get the army picture memory from. I can't check such details because all my books went with me when I joined a monastery in 1960 and didn't come out when I did in 1967, a loss I deeply regret.

Somehow or other my copy of *Animal Farm* remained with me. Signed on the half-title page with my name, and dated with the month and year it was bought, August 1953, it has a blurb on the inside front cover, headed ABOUT THIS BOOK. I take this to have been the usual style, but have no memory of ever reading a blurb as a way of helping me decide what to buy. However, it's only reasonable to suppose I did and to show how things were then as against the way they are now in blurb writing, here it is line-for-line in full:

In this good-natured satire upon dictatorship, George Orwell makes use of the technique perfected by Swift in *The Tale of a Tub*. It is the history of a revolution that went wrong—and of the excellent excuses that were forthcoming at every step for each perversion of the original doctrine.

The animals on a farm drive out their master and take over and administer the farm for themselves. The experiment is entirely successful, except for the unfortunate fact that someone has to take the deposed farmer's place. Leadership devolves almost automatically upon the pigs, who are on a higher intellectual level than the rest of the animals. Unhappily their character is not equal to their intelligence, and out of this fact springs the main development of the story. The last chapter brings a dramatic change, which, as soon as it has happened, is seen to have been inevitable from the start.

'*A very amusing and intrinsically wise book.*'
Manchester Guardian

'*This little book, about as long as* Candide, *may fairly be compared with it as a searching commentary on the dominant philosophy of the age.*'
Punch

I wish I had a diary entry that recorded whether this kind of thing had any effect on my buying, but I don't. All I certainly remember is that the biographical notes did influence me. (For instance, the information that Evelyn Waugh had converted to Roman Catholicism attracted me to his books for that reason alone.)

In the weekly ritual of selection the mid-week forays were recces, tasters. Friday was the big day. Lunchtime was spent making the final decision and purchasing the book—sometimes books, if my saved pocket money allowed it. In 1953 *Animal Farm* cost two shillings, which left me with sixpence from that week's allotment. The following week, therefore, I might have managed two books, if they were one-and-sixpence each.

Friday afternoon was always difficult. The new book was burning a hole in my desk and I was eager to get at it. As soon as school was over, I cycled home as fast as possible, went to my room and spent the hour or so until tea first admiring the outsides of the new acquisition, then going through it page by page, front to back, then reading all the extra-book matter, including the copyright page, and then trying out the first few pages to get myself used to how it was going to be but, deliberately, not enough to allow myself to be so caught that I couldn't put it down. After tea I'd usually go to the cinema. During the interval, I'd think with lusting anticipation of my new book lying on the table in my room, waiting for my return. If the film was a good one and I didn't want to spoil the pleasure of it, I'd go to bed that night without reading anything. If the film wasn't so good, I'd sit up and read my new book until I could keep awake no longer. And for the days after that the new book would be given prime-time attention until the next Friday. When I'd read it once, I entered the title and author into my list of books read and added a one-line comment. (This practice continued until I was twenty, when for some reason I left off, only to pick it up again in 1987 when I at last realized what I was missing by not keeping such a simple record.)

But I've got ahead of myself. The Great Penguin Moment mentioned earlier was the day in 1950 when I found *Sons and Lovers*. It was a Friday, and a set of books by D.H. Lawrence, of whom I had never heard, appeared all at once on the Penguin shelves. (Penguin published simultaneously one hundred thousand copies of each of ten titles by D.H Lawrence in March 1950. However, *Sons and Lovers* was not among them. Their edition of this title was first published in 1948. I can only account for my memory by guessing that, when the ten new titles came into the shop, Dressers put a copy of *Sons and Lovers* with them.) Lawrence's novel caught my eye at once because I assumed a title like that had to mean that the story had some sex in it. Please bear in mind that we are talking of the early fifties and that I was an only child who had been brought up in single-sex schools since the age of five.

Girls were difficult to get near to. Sex was a closed subject, not taught in school and not discussed at home. I was at the stage when kissing in films brought one out in a sweat. I bought *Sons and Lovers* guiltily, in the expectation of much enjoyable sweating.

I began reading that evening and didn't stop for nights on end. The effect was not at all as expected and quite as engaging as the effect of *Worzel Gummidge* five years earlier. The reason is simple. This was the first time I had read a book about myself. Till then I had thought literature was about other people. Everything that Jim Osborn had revealed fell into place. Books, literature, reading were about what happened to me, and what happened to me made a kind of sense when discovered in writing that it didn't otherwise. My own life was suddenly as alive as the life on the pages that held my mind. And it was all done with words in book-print. (Not any form of print. Magazines never meant the same, nor newspapers, nor separate sheets. It was print bound in books that did it.)

In the middle of the night when I finished my first reading of the novel I remember thinking as I turned the last page, 'I wish I had done that', meaning 'I wish I had written this book'. My next thought was, 'Why shouldn't I!' Quite consciously at that moment I decided that what I was—not wanted to be or would like to be, but *was*—was a writer. Whatever else has happened to me in the years since then, whatever else I have done or thought I might like to do, this is the one thing about which I have never wavered or doubted or changed my mind.

My encounters with Penguin weren't only private. The Grammar School library was large, run by a group of pupil librarians under the supervision of a member of staff, Percy Moss, himself an old boy of the school. Being a school librarian was taken to be an honour equivalent to being a member of the school First Fifteen rugby team or the First Eleven cricket team. I didn't know how it came about that I was invited to be a school librarian during my last two years but I was. And it was at the start of my last year that Percy asked me whether I'd like to build a Penguin library as a self-contained section of the main library. Perhaps my weekly Penguin book-buying was known about, though I never thought it was at the time.

Thereafter, every week I chose Penguins and Pelicans to the value of thirty shillings (£1.50, enough to buy ten or twelve books), made out an order, obtained a postal order for the right amount from Percy and sent them off to Penguins at Harmondsworth on the Thursday. The books arrived by post no later than the following Tuesday, when I unpacked them, entered them in a classification and accession book, reinforced their spines and the inside of the front and back covers with Sellotape, and shelved them in the Penguin section. I did this entirely on my own, only consulting Percy if I felt the need. He would look at my list each time I collected the postal order, and discuss it with me, but never interfered with my choice. I've not heard of such a thing happening in any other school, took it as normal at the time, but since then have realized that it was imaginative teaching in a school not short of such inspiration.

All in all, Penguin Books occupied a good deal of my youth, introducing me to authors I'd never heard of and books I'd not have read even if I had heard of them unless they appeared in Penguin. For in those days one somehow came to believe that anything published by Penguin was not only worth reading but ought to be read. I trusted the list completely as I trusted Jim, knowing that both would take me where I couldn't take myself, that they had my interests at heart and knew what I wanted to know. I loved Penguin books, their size, their look, their feel, their typography. They were elegant, democratic, unthreateningly attractive, affordable. I was proud of them and proud to own them. It isn't like that now. Yet, where is there another list like it still? And I only have to see one of those iconic covers, with its orange bands and characteristic sans serif lettering, for my youth to come back full-blooded, and I know again how much I owe that extraordinary publishing phenomenon. It is the embodiment of the best that my nation was, and still can be when it wants to be, but against which for the moment it has turned its back.

In Spite of Being a Translation

He was a second-year undergraduate. The group had reached the end of a three-hour seminar, the third in a course on literature for children, and were finishing off by browsing through the books that lined the room. He took one of them, *Noah Is My Name* by Maud Reuterswärd, went back to his seat and began flicking the pages. Five minutes or so later he got up, plonked the book down on a table and went off to look for something else.

When the session was over I asked what he'd thought of *Noah*. Not much, he said; it was Swedish. Was that a bad thing? Well, no, not exactly, but he didn't think any of 'our' children would like it. Why not? 'It hasn't been culturally translated.' (His words exactly.) What did he mean? The money and suchlike were all Swedish, and things happened 'we' wouldn't want to put in front of 'our' children. Such as? The little boy, seven-year-old Noah, sits on the lavatory in the bathroom and talks to his mother while she is in the bath. What's wrong with that? 'We don't do things like that! And there's an illustration of the mother in the nude holding up one of her babies while Noah watches her.' He didn't think it right for 'our' children to be shown nude women in their storybooks. And though the story is about a little boy of seven, the book didn't look at all like a book for seven-year-olds, but more like one for ten-year-olds or older, and children that age wouldn't be interested in a seven-year-old, so it wouldn't be read anyway.

Nothing would persuade him that this book had any merit or was suitable for British children. What damned it was its foreignness. Where does such prejudice come from? And who gave that nineteen-year-old student teacher the phrase 'culturally translated'? What is certain is that his attitude is not uncommon, even among older, more mature and professionally involved readers, who supposedly 'know better'. Some examples. Anthea Bell, one of our best translators from German and French (most widely known for her co-translation of the Asterix books, though I wonder how many of Asterix's British fans know her name), tells how:

> A dramatized excerpt from one of Frau Nöstlinger's books for younger children, her comic fantasy *Conrad*, was recently [1984] shown on Independent Television's *The Book Tower* programme. Apologetically, and indeed inaccurately, the presenter warned young viewers that 'this book comes from Holland', in tones so apprehensive as to suggest that foreign provenance in itself constituted good grounds for suspicion. 'But don't worry,' he more cheerfully added, 'you can read it in English.' Well, yes. That's what translations and translators are for.

The problem isn't confined to Britain. The eminent American children's publisher, Dorothy Briley, wrote:

> The words 'Translated from the...' on the title page of a book seem automatically to put it into the category of special in the minds of reviewers and buyers of children's books. Every children's book publisher knows that the label special is code for 'admire but don't buy it'. In general, translated books are a greater publishing risk than books written by English-language authors.

As a publisher of books in translation I can attest to this. Here is a sentence from a review of *A Good Hiding and Other Stories* by the much-honoured Dutch author-artist Wim Hofman, translated by Lance Salway:

> [I] would recommend [these stories] only to readers at the top of this age group (or older), not because of the language (a model of simplicity and clarity, in spite of being a translation), but because the subjects (death, nuclear war, bullying, and misunderstanding) need a more mature outlook on life.

Why 'in spite of being a translation'? And why is there nowhere in the review or the bibliographic information any mention of the name of the translator, especially since the magazine in which the review appeared is intended for school librarians? (I'll come back to the business of subject matter later.) The London *Observer*'s columnist Michael Ignatieff pointed out how rarely translators get a mention in reviews, adding:

> Theirs is an invisible profession, one that is noticed only when they get it wrong. But they are the unsung heroes of a great transformation in our culture: this opening up of our idea of where great books come from. [. . .] In the debate about multicultural education, what matters is not to confirm everybody in their ethnic, racial or gender identities, but the reverse: to take everybody out of their own skins, to take everyone on a trip into someone else's life, someone else's heart. That is what the great books do: they force us all to become translators, from the little language of what we know to the great language of what these books know.

Where children's books are concerned, it is the main English-language publishing cultures (Britain, the United States) that are the problem. Statistics for 1974 show that 30.5% of children's books published in Germany were translations. (The same year, 22.9% of belles-lettres and 1.9% of school textbooks were translations.) My impression is that this is still a fairly usual proportion, and that the same is true in other European countries. In Holland and Sweden the proportion can be as high as forty per cent. By comparison less than three per cent of British books are translations even in a good year, far less at the moment, if you leave aside international co-productions of picture books (where usually the attraction is not the few words but the dominating pictures and the commercial advantage of printing colour in large quantities). A sign of the times: in 1991 Klaus Flugge of Andersen Press, always noted for the unusual number of translated books on his list, lamented that:

> Julia MacRae, one of our most respected editors, published her last translation [...] over three years ago. As well as the demise of the hardback and the effect of library cuts, MacRae also blames a xenophobic atmosphere that she feels has developed in the last ten years [...] I have recently, reluctantly, decided to stop pub-

lishing Nöstlinger and Janosch, despite their prestigious international reputations. It is a tragedy that, out of 42 titles scheduled for 1993, Andersen Press will publish only one foreign novel this year.

The reasons for this aren't only to do with xenophobic or chauvinistic prejudices, though these are at the heart of it. When Ignatieff uses the words 'great books' he does not have in mind translations of temporarily fashionable pastime fiction. A list of 'adult' authors-in-translation we couldn't do without (not 'we' individually but our shared culture) would include the following: Aesop for his fables, the fictions of Jorge Louis Borges, Chekhov, Italo Calvino, Cervantes for *Don Quixote*, Colette, Dante for his *Inferno*, Dostoyevsky and Marguerite Duras, Flaubert, Goethe and Grass, Homer for the *Odyssey*, Ibsen for his plays, Kafka, Yasunari Kawabata, Milan Kundera, Lorca, Primo Levi, Maupassant, Molière, Harry Mulisch, Proust, the Georges Perec and Simenon, Stendhal, Tolstoy, Marguerite Yourcenar, Zola.

This is far from all. By now you're saying 'Where's—?', noticing the poor representation of women, and adding books like the Christian Bible, folktales such as those that came to us via Perrault and the Brothers Grimm, and writing by such thinkers as Plato, Kant, Schopenhauer, Wittgenstein, Simone Weil and Lao Tzu, who still influence us, all of whom come to us in translation. I've also left out the poets and scientists we can't do without. Looked at like this, we realize how much of our English-language literature isn't 'ours' at all, and how much we depend on interchange, and therefore on translation, for the liveliness, the richness, the innovative spread of our language and literature and, therefore, of our everyday life.

Play the 'great books' game with children's books. Is the outcome a comparable list? Aesop's stories, never intended to be mainly for children, have been taken over for them, as have Hans Andersen's, the Greek myths, *The Arabian Nights* and the tales of Perrault and the Brothers Grimm. Add to these the books of Jean de Brunhoff, Carlo Collodi's *Pinocchio*, Saint-Exupéry for *The Little Prince*, Selma Lagerlöf for *The Wonderful Adventures of Nils*, Tove Jansson for her glorious Moomins, Erich Kästner's *Emil and the Detectives*, Astrid Lindgren and her immortal Pippi

Longstocking, Reiner Zimnik's *The Crane*, Anne Holm's *I am David*, Alf Prøysen perhaps for Mrs Pepperpot, Johanna Spyri's *Heidi*, Johann Wyss's *Swiss Family Robinson*.

Not so impressive, and weighted towards folk and fairy tales not originally considered to be 'children's'. More women though, as you'd expect of the Cinderella of literary production. Are we to suppose, then, that there is a list of universal 'greats' that haven't been translated into English? Are the Germans and Dutch, French and Italians, Spanish and Greeks, Norwegians and Hungarians, Russians and Slovenians all sharing a children's library of classics we know nothing about? I doubt it.

The fact is that the development, beginning in the eighteenth century, of the children's book into an art form in its own right, rather than merely a didactic tool, has been dominated in quantity and in durability by the Anglo-American English-language nexus. Some languages still have no rich production of books for the young; others started much later than the English. It is a strange rule-of-thumb that countries in the cold and temperate climates are big producers for children and that the warmer the climate gets the less children's publishing there is. Another north-south divide. There are deep cultural reasons as well as economic explanations. And things are changing rapidly. The Italians who, despite *Pinocchio*, have nothing to compare historically with English children's literature, are currently very busy building up their publishing in that sector (and buying a lot of translation rights from other languages). On the other hand, I wonder what has gone on in Russia, with its long tradition of writing for the young. There was a children's department in the publishing house Parus as early as 1916, somewhat before any such editorial specialism in Britain. Kornei Chukovsky was head of it then. Later he wrote many children's stories, mostly in verse, a form very popular in Russia, becoming so loved because of them that he was known nationally by adults and children alike as Uncle Chukasha, a familiarity that protected him when, near the end of his life, he assisted Solzhenitsyn during his persecution. He also wrote *From Two to Five*, one of the classic studies of children's language and story, available in English only in an unsatisfactory American translation. In it he championed the importance of fairy and nonsense tales at a time when it was politically incorrect, not to say dangerous to do so.

Nevertheless, it's true, I think, that there isn't a bookcase full of great untranslated children's books waiting to be brought to us in English. What is true, however, is that we are denied in English a significant number of books that are the best recently published and currently being published in other languages. When David Turton and I set up the Turton & Chambers imprint in 1989 specifically to publish translations, and I began looking carefully at what was available in Dutch, the Scandinavian languages, German and French, I couldn't understand why the writers we went on to publish—Peter Pohl, Ted van Lieshout, Wim Hofman, Joke van Leeuwen, Imme Dros, Maud Reuterswärd, Gert Loschütz and Claude Gutman—hadn't already come to us, and why no more than one of Tormod Haugen's books had been translated (*The Night Birds*, published by Collins in 1985 and out of print). These are authors working at a level that matches anything written by any of our own, and they have all produced work that in nature and technique extends the range of literature for child and young adult readers. Some are so far ahead in subject matter or treatment that one of the reasons why, so I'm told, they haven't been translated is that English-language publishers are afraid the content would cause too much upset and thus suffer even lower sales than translations usually achieve.

Here then is the dilemma. There is no point in translating books of a kind that merely add to a very large number we already produce for ourselves. Why, for example, translate a run-of-the-mill teenage romance when we already have more than enough home-grown? We are awash with mediocrity without importing more.

Equally, there is no point in translating books of a kind we do very well unless they add something to the genre. We have in English a long, universally admired tradition of talking-animal stories, some of which are classics. Think of *The Wind in the Willows* and *The Just-So Stories*. *Winnie-the-Pooh* extends the type into talking-toy-animal stories and Ted Hughes extends the form in another direction with *What is the Truth?* The range and quality (however defined) are impressive. Anything translated must match this. Nothing I have come across so far in other languages does, with the exception perhaps of the Dutchman Toon

Tellegen's recent work.

Then there is the problem of content, already mentioned. One of the things that makes books from other cultures so interesting is that their view of the world is a little different from our own—a different perspective, a different set of attitudes and assumptions, not least assumptions about what is all right for children to know and read about. They take us, as Michael Ignatieff puts it, 'out of our own skins [...] on a trip into someone else's life'—a life culturally different from ours. And it is the difference that matters. This is a primary value, a principal reason for choosing to translate a book. And yet ideological taboos, the protective screens we erect around children, cause resistance. Remember the undergraduate and the scene in which Noah talks to his mother while she is naked in the bath: 'We don't do things like that!' (As with all criticism, this tells us more about the critic than the book. He also fell into the familiar trap of presuming to speak for all his compatriots by generalizing into 'we' the reactions entirely to do with himself alone.) I have in front of me right now ten books I believe should be published in English, all of them considered in their countries of origin to be superlative examples of literature for young readers, the best being produced at the moment. But I know they would sell very few copies—far too few to pay off anywhere near their production costs—because they combine what would be regarded in Britain, America and (less severely) Australia as subject matter that is 'too risky' and narrative forms that are too unusual (always called 'difficult' by nervous, narrow-ranged readers).

The encouraging thing is that these boundaries are not fixed, but do change, gradually most of the time, quite rapidly now and then. Despite the problems of the kind I've mentioned, and others not yet touched on, I do believe that in Britain and especially in Australia, there are signs that more and more teachers and librarians are concerned about our isolationist tendency, our prejudice against 'the foreign', and are prepared to do something about it. Indeed, the British national curriculum requires that children be exposed to literature from other cultures. But if anything that matters is to be done about it, the books must be available in sufficient diversity to appeal to a variety of readers' needs and experience, and the enabling adults—teachers and librarians in particular—must know about them.

It is writing and publishing books that are 'different', that have a voice and a manner of telling of their own, a distinctness of personality and thought, that interest me. The problems are considerable, but the attempt is essential.

Now for the difficulties of translating itself. Think of a story as apparently simple and straightforward as a fable. Here is Lev Vygotsky in *Thought and Language*:

> In translating the fable 'The Grasshopper and the Ant', Krylov substituted a dragonfly for La Fontaine's grasshopper. In French, *grasshopper* is feminine and therefore well suited to symbolize a lighthearted, carefree attitude. The nuance would be lost in a literal translation, since in Russian *grasshopper* is masculine. When he settled for *dragonfly*, which is feminine in Russian, Krylov disregarded the literal meaning in favor of the grammatical form required to render La Fontaine's thought. [...] One grammatical detail may, on occasion, change the whole purport of what is said.

Anthea Bell, who believes that 'it is the spirit rather than the letter that the translator pursues', explains just how problematic even apparently small matters can be to the spirit of a text:

> Take tense; take in particular that interesting tense the historic present. English does not, like the languages from which I chiefly translate, leap nimbly from historic present to past and back again as a narrative method. Once you have committed yourself to the historic present in continuous narrative you are more or less stuck with it, and with getting all other tenses (such as conditionals) into line with it, unless you are going to be experimental, which is no part of a translator's duty unless reflecting the experimental nature of an author's original work. There are not many differences in approach between translating children's and adult literature, but I do find this is one of them [...]
>
> Those tiny parts of speech, pronouns, can be trickiest of all. English is a language which has lost grammatical gender;

> French and German have not. Obvious, of course, but therefore, if you must assign 'he', 'she' or 'it' to a noun which has grammatical gender in the original (and automatically takes a pronoun to match) but has no built-in gender in English, you are inevitably loading the whole idea with extra significance. [...Take] the sun and the moon. We tend to think of the moon as feminine; our poets have thought of it that way for centuries. *The Concise Oxford Dictionary* unhesitatingly defines 'she' as 'The female (or thing personified as female, e.g. the moon...) previously mentioned'. But when we still had grammatical gender, back in Anglo-Saxon times, moon was masculine and sun feminine, as is still the case in German. When we lost grammatical gender, why did we decide the moon was feminine and the sun masculine? [...] But to the Germans [...] Sun is still feminine in a folktale context, and the Moon masculine, with pronouns to match, so that where Ludwig Bechstein in the nineteenth century collected one of the glass mountain tales (of our British 'Black Bull of Norroway' type) and the king's daughter must visit the Sun and the Moon, who are making chicken soup, to beg the chicken bones from which she can build a ladder to help her up the mountainside, Bechstein's twentieth-century illustrator provides a picture of a warmly golden, very female, matronly Sun.

Magnify such a seemingly small detail many times and we begin to sense the linguistic and stylistic problems buried in every fictional text when making a faithful translation. But what is a 'faithful translation'? Anthea Bell claims it has to do with the spirit of the original not the literal sense. Horace said a translator should not try to render the original word for word like an obedient *interpres* (negotiator) but should work from sense to sense. Erasmus, in the preface to his New Testament, argued that

> Language consists of two parts, namely words and meaning, which are like body and soul. If both of them can be rendered I do not object to word for word translation. If they cannot, it would be preposterous for a translator to keep the words and deviate from the meaning.

Contrarily, in an essay central to the subject, 'The Task of the Translator', Walter Benjamin struggles with the difficulty of how far literalness, how far freedom, and argues for literalness, concluding:

> [I]t is not the highest praise of a translation, particularly in the age of its origin, to say that it reads as if it had originally been written in that language. Rather, the significance of fidelity as ensured by literalness is that the work reflects the great longing for linguistic complementation. A real translation is transparent; it does not cover the original, does not block its light, but allows the pure language, as though reinforced by its own medium, to shine upon the original all the more fully. This may be achieved, above all, by a literal rendering of the syntax which proves words rather than sentences to be the primary element of the translator. For if the sentence is the wall before the language of the original, literalness is the arcade.

This was a view shared at an even greater extreme by Robert Browning, who thought, John Addington Symonds records in his diary, that translation 'Ought to be absolutely literal, with exact rendering of words, and words placed in the order of the original'. Many readers will be surprised by such a preference, one of the complaints often made by people who dislike translated books being that 'they read like translations'.

These opinions and many others are examined in *The Poetics of Translation: History, Theory, Practice* by Willis Barnstone, a comprehensive study that leaves one agreeing mightily with Wilhelm Humbolt's comment in a letter to August Wilhelm Schlegel, 'All translation seems to me simply an attempt to accomplish an impossible task', while at the same time echoing Schlegel in *Translating Literature*, 'The human mind can do nothing but translate; all its activity consists of just that.'

All this and a lot more must happen before the publisher's editor gets her hands on the text, when extra-textual impediments may be encountered as well.

Of the many gatherings of people interested in children's books held every year, few give time to the subject of translation. One that devoted all its time to it was the Third Symposium of the International Research Society for Children's Literature, held in Sweden in 1976. In her paper 'How Emil Becomes Michel', Birgit Stolt offered a number of examples of the influence, if not the interference, of editors in the translation process. She told, for example, of a story by Astrid Lindgren about little Lotta

> who yearns to grow up very quickly. She had heard that dung and rain hasten growth and on a rainy day she stands in the middle of a dung-heap and thinks that she will now grow big very quickly. In the American translation Astrid Lindgren discovered to her great surprise that the dung-heap had turned into a pile of withered leaves! This time she wrote to the publishers and asked whether American children really did not know that there were other means, much better than withered leaves, of hastening growth. If it were not so, she didn't think much of American agriculture. This time she was successful: 'I was allowed to keep my dung-heap—what a triumph!' she writes.

On another occasion Lindgren wasn't so successful, this time with the French edition of *Pippi Longstocking*, in which Pippi is not allowed to pick up a horse, only a pony, because, the publisher insisted, Swedish children might be persuaded that a girl was strong enough to lift a horse, but that 'French children, who had just been through a World War, were much too realistic to be taken in by something like that'.

These are merely tasters of what could be an anthology of anecdotes to which anyone whose fiction has been translated inevitably has a story to contribute. In her paper Birgit Stolt identifies 'three sources which may adversely affect the faithfulness' of the translation of an original text intended for child readers:

> 1. Educational intentions. [By which she means cutting out passages and words thought too difficult; cutting out or changing passages that might offend moral or other guardians; adding information because children might not understand the story otherwise; and so on.]
>
> 2. The preconceived opinion of adults about what children

want to read, value, and understand. It often goes together with an underestimation of the child reader.

3. The sentimentalization or prettifying of matter-of-fact texts. ['Astrid Lindgren,' Stolt writes, 'speaks of the ambition of many a translator to make everything a bit more beautiful and more full of genuine feeling than the author has succeeded in making it'.]

It is my own experience as translated writer and publisher that translators and editors tend to flatten a text by rendering in conventional, familiar language an author's quirkiness—oddities of diction or image, unusualness of narrative voice, shifts of person or tense, unexpected elisions that deliberately leave awkward indeterminacies, ungrammatical constructions, and the like. And though they often explain this by claiming the 'difficulty' is 'impossible' to translate, one sometimes catches a glimpse of another unstated reason, which is a fear that, if they devise similar oddities in their own language, critics and readers who do not or cannot check the original will judge these to be translator's errors and will quote them as examples of mistaken or inept use of the host language.

One of the best analyses of the impulses of translators that I know of is Milan Kundera's *Testaments Betrayed*, where he itemizes what translators have done to Kafka. At one point he discusses what he calls 'systematic synonymizing', an example of the problem I have just mentioned:

> The need to use another word in place of the more obvious, more simple, more neutral one [. . .] may be called the *synonymizing reflex* —a reflex of nearly all translators. Having a great stock of synonyms is a feature of 'good style' virtuosity; if the word 'sadness' appears twice in the same paragraph of the original text, the translator, offended by the repetition (considered an attack on obligatory style elegance), will be tempted to translate the second occurrence as 'melancholy'. But there's more: this need to synonymize is so deeply embedded in the translator's soul that he will choose a synonym *first off*: he'll say 'melancholy' if the original text has 'sadness' and 'sadness' if the original has 'melancholy'.

> We concede with no irony whatever: the translator's situation is extremely delicate: he must keep faith with the author and at the same time remain himself; what to do? He wants (consciously or unconsciously) to invest the text with his own creativity; as if to give himself heart, he chooses a word that does not obviously betray the author but still arises from his own initiative. I am noticing this right now as I look over the translation of a small text of mine: I write 'author', and the translator translates it 'writer'; I write 'writer', and he translates it 'novelist'; I write 'novelist', and he translates it 'author'; where I say 'verse', he says 'poetry'; where I say 'poetry', he says 'poems'. Kafka says 'go', the translators, 'walk'. Kafka says 'no element', the translators: 'none of the elements', 'no longer anything', 'not a single element'. This practice of synonymization seems innocent, but its systematic quality inevitably smudges the original idea. And besides, what the hell for? Why not 'go' when the author says '*gehen*'? O ye translators, do not sodonymize us!

In another passage he sums up the problem:

> For a translator, the supreme authority should be the *author's personal style*. But most translators obey another authority: that of the *conventional version* of 'good French' (or good German, good English, etc.), namely, the French (German, etc.) we learn in school. The translator considers himself the ambassador from that authority to the foreign author. That is the error: every author of some value *transgresses* against 'good style', and in that transgression lies the originality (and hence the raison d'être) of his art. The translator's primary effort should be to understand that transgression. This is not difficult when it is obvious, as for example with Rabelais, or Joyce, or Céline. But there are authors whose transgression against 'good style' is subtle, barely visible, hidden, discreet; as such, it is not easy to grasp. In such a case, it is all the more important to do so.

Of course, I quote this passage because I agree with it. But I also accept, as Kundera remarks, that translators can never be neutral. Like writers, they are individuals, with their own idiosyncrasies of language and personality that inevitably flavour their work, aside from the fact that, just as there are bad writers, there are bad translators. Which is why choice of translator for a particular text is so important; even the best may be right for one sort but not for another. And in publishing for children this choice is itself made even harder by the fact that translators are usually paid less for translating a children's text than they are a text for adults, which limits the choice to the very few good ones who happen to be dedicated to the task.

'Either the translator leaves the author in peace as much as possible and moves the reader towards him', wrote Schleiermacher in 1813, 'or he leaves the reader in peace as much as possible and moves the author towards him.' The danger is that in a tussle between the two we end up with a mixture of both, of translation and 'adaptation', which, Schleiermacher rightly warned, results in 'the author and reader completely missing each other.' The instinct among children's book editors is to leave the reader in peace and move the author; my own preference is for moving the reader. It is the difference of an author that matters, the difference of a book. How young readers are brought to them—how they are encouraged to enjoy difference—is a matter for educators, librarians, parents, and other adult enablers, not for translators, whose task is to be faithful to the author and the text.

In between are publishers, who make decisions about a book's suitability for its supposed audience and how far they want to go in offering the new and unfamiliar. But even for publishers, in my view, responsibility to the author and to the book should be primary. If their concerns for the audience are so great as to require significant adaptation of a book—the smoothing out of peculiarities, whether of form, language or content—better to leave the book untranslated than warp and adulterate it.

The most demanding book I've worked on editorially is *Johnny, my friend* (*Janne, min vän*) by the Swedish author Peter Pohl, translated for the Turton & Chambers imprint by Laurie Thompson. Some of the difficulties it presents and the solutions we chose in resolving them illustrate the interest as well as the complexities and difficulties of translation.

Johnny, my friend is problematic in content, form and language.

It is also long, which increases the cost of production as well of translation. Set in the 1950s not only in a particular area of Stockholm that has its own peculiarities of colloquial speech, but in and around a particular and well-known high school (still functioning in the same building), it is a story about just-adolescent boys which, judged by the old-fashioned coding of such narratives, has many qualities of a story about girls; indeed, gender is at the heart of its mystery. And it is a mystery, a detective story—a murder is being investigated; identity of victim, murderer(s), and their motive are in question; clues must be found and pieced together to make a coherent whole from a telling that moves back and forth in the chronology of the tale. Yet it is also quite as considerably a story about friendship and love, about school and family, about conflicting loyalties, about thought and 'knowing things', about growing out of what you have been and becoming what you most feel you are; and more. In its way of telling, its linguistic and narrative devices, Pohl deploys with great skill and density a number of techniques, of both narrative and typography, not usually found in fiction for early adolescents. It is an entirely modern novel.

Put simply, in my judgement, *Janne, min vän* is a rare masterpiece. I know of no other contemporary 'older children's book' that betters it and few, whether for children or adults, that match it. As do all great novels, it transcends descriptive or categorizing labels and, as Kundera suggests is always the case with books of 'some value', it transgresses conventional norms. In Sweden, where it was first published in 1985, it is much honoured, treasured and discussed. In Germany it received close attention and the valued Youth Literature Prize. In the Netherlands it was greeted with enthusiastic admiration. In Australia it was favourably but not exceptionally noticed in the specialist children's book journals. In Britain it received one tepid review. By mid 1996, five years after English-language publication, no publisher has brought it out in the USA. A great book that epitomizes the chauvinist declension.

I first came across it when a copy of the Swedish edition was given me by a young Swedish friend, Katarina Kuick, now a professional writer and my own translator. *Janne, min vän*, she told me, was one of the two most important books of adolescence she knew and though I couldn't read it she wanted me to have a copy. She told me the story and wrote a long synopsis for me as well, and explained what it was that meant so much to her—partly the story itself, partly the way of telling. She knew the text inside out.

When Turton & Chambers began, I knew I wanted to publish an English edition; in fact, anger that such an extraordinary novel hadn't appeared in English was a key factor in my decision to be part of T&C in the first place. After negotiating rights with its Swedish publisher, I visited the author, taking Katarina along to help with any language difficulties (Pohl's English is modest, my Swedish nonexistent), and because she knew the text. Together we had prepared a list of questions a translator would need to settle and had discussed how to put them to Pohl, a researcher in mathematics as well as an author who is notoriously reserved about inquiries into his writing and especially about questions to do with the tell-tale gaps, the indeterminacies, in *Janne*. He refused the usual publisherly blandishments of lunch or dinner in some smart restaurant, preferring instead to meet over dispenser-machine coffee in the staff common room of his department at the university. I warmed to him for that; throughout the conversation he showed an admirable distaste for time-wasting and bullshit. He and Katarina got along well (no author can resist, I suppose, a reader who knows his books intimately); that Pohl knew some of my own novels helped to establish our common interest in the possibilities of form and the importance of how the text looks on the page. Most of our questions were answered, and Pohl explained details in the text about which he felt strongly.

One of our questions concerned dialogue and how it should be treated typographically, another was the use of italics. Pohl didn't want dialogue to be indicated by inverted commas, as in the English convention, or by the dash, as in continental European convention. He had been careful to construct a style that blended dialogue and narrative, and direct and reported speech, in such a mesh that they formed one 'voice' and yet, he was sure, any reader competent enough to read his book would also be competent enough to understand which was speech between characters and which was interior monologue or narrative commentary. Unfortunately, the Swedish edition was not consistent; sometimes dialogue had been marked by punctuation. An example, this, of how editorial decisions or mistakes in an originating edition are carried over into a translated edition, unless the author's intentions can be checked. In the same way, apt equivalents can be found for many details which at first seem 'untranslatable' if the author and translator work together. I've learned this with my own books, and have been pleased by the amount that can thus be 'saved'.

As for the use of italics, this was confined to one feature of the text: the moments when the narrator-protagonist is speaking in his mind to Janne during the time the story is being told (as against the time the scene is taking place). So italics could not be used for, say, emphasis. When he wanted emphasis Pohl employed the German convention of spaced lettering, as in h e l p. Though I could foresee awkward typesetting problems (such as when a stretched word came at the end of a line and spilled over into the next), I readily agreed to it (indeed, I liked it and wished I'd thought of using it in my own books).

We also talked about more usual problems like the names of characters, and of streets, all of them real streets and often plot-significant in relation to each other. Many English-language readers dislike translations because of 'names you can't say'; three-barrelled names in Russian literature are usually cited. In *Janne, min vän* the central narrating character is called Krille, which is not a name familiar to English-language eyes. Chris is a possible English equivalent. I was anxious that young readers should not be disconcerted by characters' names when I knew they would have to face other textual unfamiliarities of a fairly complex order. So my opinion, though reluctant, was that we should anglicize any names that were totally unfamiliar but retain any that were readable and recognizable, such as Krille's street friend, Pecka. Katarina was very against this, wanting to retain all the Swedish names because, she said, it was time English readers got used to this, just as Swedish children were used to it in books from other languages. Pohl didn't mind. He wanted English readers to feel comfortable in this respect.

However, the question of names isn't always as straightforward as that. In my own novel, *The Toll Bridge*, for example, the central male character is called Jan, a name which in English is ambivalent, being either male (Jan Needle) or more usually female (Jan Mark). The ambivalence in my novel is intended. But in Dutch Jan is an extremely common male name, and not likely to be thought significantly ambivalent. It was right, therefore, to find a Dutch name that would 'work' as Jan does in English. But just to complicate matters, Jan in the story is a diminutive of Janus and not a version of Janet, say, or John. So a root name was needed that would allow both Jan and Janus. The translator chose Jany. In Pohl's book this same problem beset us with Krille's mysterious friend Janne. At first everyone thinks Janne is a boy, but later on we realize he might be a girl, and the name Janne in Swedish would allow this confusion. To have called him Jan in English would, as I've suggested, allow too easy an assumption that the character is female. So what name to use? I settled on Johnny, a decision I've never been entirely happy with.

The fact is you cannot make a blanket rule about never changing names when translating. Names in stories often have symbolic or other associated meanings which help determine the narrative's deeper meanings, and translators must try and retain these, which will sometimes require a change of name between one language and another.

The street names in *Janne* are even 'harder' for young English readers than the characters' names—a couple of them, topped with the dots and circle that distinguish two of the three extra letters in the Swedish alphabet, take up (in the English edition) almost the whole of the sixth line of the first page: Swedenborgsgatan and Maria Prästgårdsgata. Could they be anglicized? Did they matter so much that they couldn't be removed? They mattered a lot, Katarina said. The plot was carefully worked out, not just street by street but building by building; it would be sacrilege to remove them, and anglicizing would make a nonsense of them—the characters might be 'fiction' but the streets were *there*.

It then occurred to me that both Pohl and Katarina were assuming that everyone would know the streets, their layout and relationship. Naturally, because both were Stockholmites, both had attended the very school used in the book, and like all natives they assumed strangers would easily find their way around (strangers are always told, when asking directions of a native, 'You can't miss it'). What we strangers needed was a map. Then we'd see that the story is set in a real place and be able to trace the movements of the characters if we wanted to, and—the important point—maps somehow do make strange names and unfamiliar places easier to manage. (An added advantage is that young readers tend to like maps in stories; maps seem to increase the sense of adventure.) This is why the English edition is the only one so far that starts the story with a map of Krille/Chris's area of Stockholm.

But even maps make problems. Should we reproduce the relevant section from an official street map of the period? (No: too detailed and cluttered.) Should it be drawn in the way Krille/Chris himself would have drawn it, the cartographic equivalent of his first-person narrative? (An attractive idea at first thought.) Or should it be drawn diagrammatically, like the map of the London Underground? (No: easy to follow but anachronistic.) Should it be to scale? How much detail should it contain? And so on. In the end it was drawn by a friend of Katarina's who was good at graphics but not so good that the result would look like a studio production; the amateurishness suits the pretence that this is Krille/Chris's book but it is clear and detailed enough to tell readers all they need to know.

After I'd discussed the book with Pohl and Katarina, the translator was chosen. Laurie Thompson also visited Pohl before producing a sample translation of the first few pages of the novel so that we could agree his treatment of the first-person style. In his covering letter, Laurie wrote:

> [The] problem is hitting the right level of colloquialism: Chris speaks informally, but in much better style than the rest of the gang —and he occasionally waxes formal. As always, there are frequently no direct English equivalents for individual slang words and phrases, so it is often a case of trying to give the whole paragraph a similar tone rather than worrying too much about specific phrases. I'm trying to remember the kind of colloquialisms current when I was at school [in the 1950s, when the story is set], while avoiding giving too dated an impression.

Katarina combed the sample, making numerous comparative comments on the Swedish and English texts which I found extremely useful. Here demonstrated is one of the problems that make publishing of translations so distasteful to many editors, and may be one of the reasons why there are few in English children's books. When an editor is not familiar with the original language she feels inadequate in her editorial role. Normally, when dealing with an author in her own language, an editor is confident about making suggestions or challenging the author's meaning or use of language. But if the editor isn't fluent in the original language how can she challenge the authority of the translator? Thus the editor's own uneasiness with a language becomes part of the resistance to publishing translations. And British editors are notoriously ignorant of other languages. Most can manage some of one, usually French or German. By contrast, my Dutch editor is at home in five languages, my German in four and they are not unusual among their continental European colleagues.

A typically English monolinguist myself, I was determined that my ignorance wouldn't inhibit me. The only way I could think of to give myself the informed confidence I needed was to take on an original language consultant, such as Katarina, whose English is fluent, and to make sure that she worked closely with me on the text, though leaving me to make the editorial decisions and to deal with the translator. Naturally, this increases the cost of production. Of course, not all translations present the range of problems or require the exceptional attention of *Janne, min vän*, but if they do a publishing structure is there to cope with them and the translators know that their work will receive close editorial scrutiny, not something that every translator into English is used to or welcomes, having so often been deferred to as an unchallengeable authority. With translators, my experience is that the usual rule applies: the people best at their job give the least trouble and are easiest to work with.

Something of the resulting process of consultation, comparison of Swedish and English, making of editorial suggestions, redrafting by the translator, further editorial revision, final draft, and first published text of *Johnny, my friend* can be sampled by comparing three versions of the book's first page. Figure 1 is the beginning of Laurie Thompson's first trial draft. Figure 2 is my edited version of Laurie's second draft of the same passage. Figure 3 is the first page of the published book. (All are facsimiles reduced in size from the originals.)

A few points. 'Cop' was used in preference to Laurie's choice of 'bobby' because 'bobby' has a familiar, even neighbourhood-friendly feel, whereas 'cop' has a harder edge and in the early 1950s would have been thought by people of Chris's age more gutsy and tough-guy glamorous (the influence of Hollywood crime movies). Changing 'respond with' to 'flash', the insertion of 'at each other' and changing 'wants' to 'feels the urge' were intended to move the text closer to the original in meaning and flavour. The change of Stan to Sten resulted from Katarina's continuing argument that Swedish names should be retained as far as possible. The changes in the fourth paragraph—'With little movements...'—were mostly to do with clarifying the action and moving the text closer to the original in style.

The sentence after the line break, 'You got to know Johnny by his bicycle', presented a problem we never quite solved. Katarina insisted that the meaning of the original is rather like 'you met Johnny by bicycle', suggesting he was inseparable from his cycle, that you met him while cycling, and that you 'knew' him 'through' cycling (as Laurie first expressed it), a phrasing I didn't find convincing in English. Laurie, quite rightly, was unhappy with my suggestion 'You got to know Johnny by cycle', seen in Figure 2. It doesn't really work in English either. We settled for 'You got to know Johnny by his bicycle' because that chimed with the cop producing the bicycle in the first sentence of the book—a piece of evidence and a clue that causes the gang to 'flash the whites of their eyes at each other'. But none of us was satisfied with the solution; it loses too much.

It would be right to think that every page received this amount of attention but wrong to think that every page required so many changes. Laurie did an exceptionally difficult job with great skill and patience. Katarina was especially useful because of her close knowledge of the peculiar nuances and colloquialisms of Chris's area of Stockholm, because of her passionate commitment to the original and its subtleties, and her rapport with the author, which helped us clarify some of the deliberate indeterminacies of the plot so that we could be sure of the intended level of mystification about which, in public, Pohl can be even more mystifying. As for me, I'm proud of the achievement and of making such a fine

1

Now then lads, does any of you recognize this? says the bobby, picking up Johnny's bicycle.

The whole gang responds with the whites of their eyes, but nobody feels called on to volunteer. The bobby's mate is still sitting there in the cop car, wittering away about the corner of Swedenborgsgatan and Maria Prästgårdsgata into his mike. About ten young lads. I'll get back to you.

The bobby's eyes settle on Stan, but Stan's having problems with his shoe laces, enormous problems; Stan's shoelaces are taking up all his attention. There's something wrong with Pecka's belt as well: his belt has got snarled up all of a sudden, you know how it is. Harold is helping him to sort it out — good old Harold, you can trust him to be nice to his kid brother.

With a series of little movements, so little they'd be unobtrusive if they weren't so obvious, everybody in the gang is busy adjusting things. Turning this way. Turning that way. Turning the other way. All their little adjustments combine to form a stage, and in the middle of that stage is me, with an audience of one: the bobby. Everybody else has something else to look at. The whole audience wants to know if I — nobody else, just me — recognize Johhny's bicycle.

Do I recognize Johnny's bicycle!

That's how we got to know Johnny, through his bicycle. Half past six on the last day of August in my case, 18.32, 31.08.1954. The summer holidays had just petered out, and school — a new school as far as I was concerned, known to everybody as South Side Grammar — had started at half past one that afternoon. An easy-going sort of start with a roll call and a parade in the hall, featuring ancient, shaggy gents with walking sticks and ear trumpets and gravelly coughs and a whole waiting room of aches and pains, each of 'em with one and a half feet in the grave. Our future teachers, in other words.

At half past six we all came riding down various streets on our bicycles, in my case down St. Paulsgatan, and it's my case I'm talking about now. Aimed a few quick shots over our shoulders, ducked down to avoid the volleys fired back from the doorways, and turned off suddenly in the last direction the car drivers could have imagined. They all had to ram on their brakes: after all, we were the young hopefuls, the guardians of Sweden's future, who had to survive today's traffic in order

Figure 1
Translator's first draft of the first page of *Johnny, my friend*

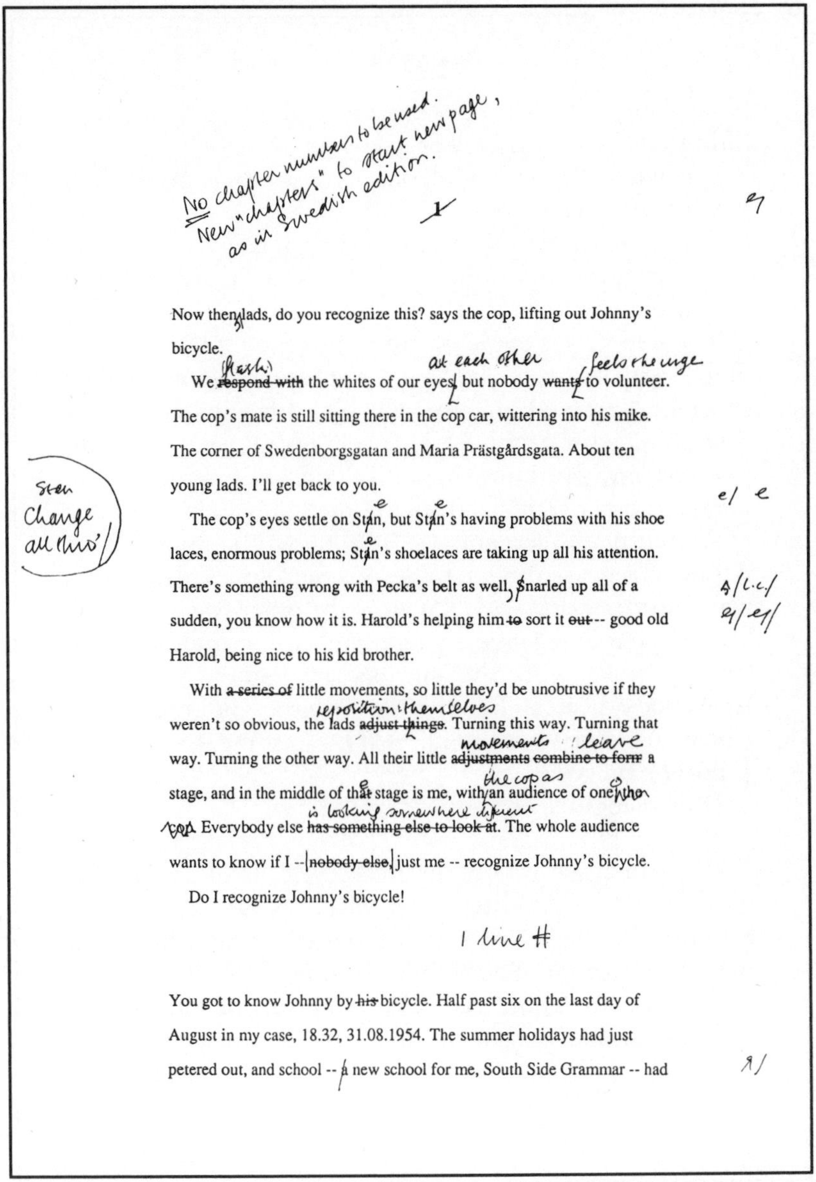

No chapter numbers to be used. New "chapters" to start new page, as in Swedish edition.

1

Now then, lads, do you recognize this? says the cop, lifting out Johnny's bicycle.

We respond with the whites of our eyes, but nobody wants to volunteer. The cop's mate is still sitting there in the cop car, wittering into his mike. The corner of Swedenborgsgatan and Maria Prästgårdsgata. About ten young lads. I'll get back to you.

The cop's eyes settle on Stan, but Stan's having problems with his shoe laces, enormous problems; Stan's shoelaces are taking up all his attention. There's something wrong with Pecka's belt as well, Snarled up all of a sudden, you know how it is. Harold's helping him to sort it out -- good old Harold, being nice to his kid brother.

With a series of little movements, so little they'd be unobtrusive if they weren't so obvious, the lads adjust things. Turning this way. Turning that way. Turning the other way. All their little adjustments combine to form a stage, and in the middle of that stage is me, with an audience of one, the cop. Everybody else has something else to look at. The whole audience wants to know if I -- nobody else, just me -- recognize Johnny's bicycle.

Do I recognize Johnny's bicycle!

You got to know Johnny by his bicycle. Half past six on the last day of August in my case, 18.32, 31.08.1954. The summer holidays had just petered out, and school -- a new school for me, South Side Grammar -- had

Figure 2
Edited version of the second draft of *Johnny, my friend*

Now then, lads, do you recognize this? says the cop, lifting out Johnny's bicycle.

We flash the whites of our eyes at each other, but nobody feels the urge to volunteer. The cop's mate is still sitting there in the cop car, wittering into his mike. The corner of Swedenborgsgatan and Maria Prästgårdsgata. About ten young lads. I'll get back to you.

The cop's eyes settle on Sten, but Sten's having problems with his shoe laces, enormous problems; Sten's shoelaces are taking up all his attention. There's something wrong with Pecka's belt as well, snarled up all of a sudden, you know how it is. Harold's giving him a hand – good old Harold, being nice to his kid brother.

With little movements, so little they'd be unobtrusive if they weren't so obvious, the lads regroup. Turning this way. Turning that way. Turning the other way. All their little movements leave a stage, and in the middle of the stage is me, with the cop as an audience of one. Everybody else is looking somewhere different. The whole audience wants to know if I – just me – recognize Johnny's bicycle.

Do I recognize Johnny's bicycle!

You got to know Johnny by his bicycle. Half past six on the last day of August in my case, 18.32, 31.08.1954. Summer holidays had just petered out, and school – a new school for me, South Side Grammar – had got going 13.30 that afternoon. An easy-going sort of start with a roll call and a parade in the hall, featuring ancient,

9

Figure 3
First page of published *Johnny, my friend*

book available in English. I am not, however, any more optimistic about the future for translations into English than I was in 1989. The sales of Turton & Chambers books have been so poor that we cannot afford to go on publishing. In the last two or three years fewer translations than ever have been published in the UK.

How to improve this distressing state of affairs? Publishers tend to follow markets as well as create them. Which means that main buyers of children's books—teachers and librarians—can have an effect. They can begin by raising awareness of books in translation, showing young readers well-known books from other languages, bringing translators into classrooms and libraries to give talks, and generally highlighting this sector of literature. Reviewers and critics might pay more considered attention to translations and to the work of translation. (How many reviews ever comment on this, unless in disparaging terms like the one quoted earlier?) Some moves are afoot. A new award in recognition of translated books for children, the Marsh Prize, given for the first time in 1996, will be made every other year. And, not to be ignored, the national curriculum requires that children be made aware of books from other countries and cultures.

All of which means that we must tackle our own as well as other adults' prejudices about translation and books that are 'different' (whether translations or not) by attending carefully to them and discovering in difference a virtue rather than an impediment.

Something *Zeppelin*!

It is a great satisfaction as well as an honour to be with you, celebrating the work of Tormod Haugen. Besides being the first English-language publisher of *Zeppelin* and a teacher of children's literature, I am also a fiction writer, whose novel *Dance on my Grave* was translated into Norwegian by Tormod, for which I now have an opportunity to thank him face-to-face. So I have a triple view of *Zeppelin*: as a publisher, as a teacher and as an author-and-reader. What I want to tell you, then, is a story about the discovery of a book and the reasons I wanted to publish it in translation; a story about one reader's reading of it and his view of its place in the children's literature of today; and a story about the book's reception by adults and children in three English-language countries.

As you know, the British are notoriously resistant to books in translation, especially so with children's books. In 1989 an Australian business friend, David Turton, and I decided to try to do something about this by setting up a small independent publisher, Turton & Chambers, and I was buying rights in books I had come across while visiting countries where I'd been invited to talk about my own novels in translation.

One of these countries was Sweden, where a young reader who had become a friend and is now my Swedish translator as well, Katarina Kuick, had already drawn my attention to Peter Pohl's masterpiece *Janne, min vän*, which I am proud to have made available in English. It was Katarina who also alerted me to *Zeppelin*. As I am monolingual, she had to do what readers always do for nonreaders: she told me the story, translated a few passages and explained why she thought it was worth the trouble and expense of publishing in English. Like so much else in life, publishing is about difficult choices, about deciding what matters to you and what doesn't, about making value judgements. Publishers, librarians, teachers make value judgements on behalf of other people. They can't avoid it, it's their job.

What I was looking for, I had told Katarina and consultants in other countries, were books that represented the best being written for young readers in their language of origin, that were at the forefront, the growing point, of the literature, and were the kind of books I'd like to have written myself. From all I heard, first from Katarina, then from others who knew Norwegian children's books, *Zeppelin* fitted these criteria. As Katarina explained in a letter:

> The book is told in a kind of dreamlike way. Nina is not fully aware of what is happening at the beginning, nor whether the boy is real or not, dangerous or friendly, but she grows and in the end takes the initiative, even challenges and wins over her father. Whether the boy is going to return or not is left open. The story is close to fairytale in some respects, yet is very realistic, and the portrait of Nina's family is very well drawn. The unspoken conflicts, the smiling surfaces, Nina's role as the angel, a role she hasn't chosen and doesn't want. It's a very revealing book, showing the grown-ups as the small figures they really are. I liked it. More and more, actually [. . .] The book definitely grows on you as you think about it. It doesn't go away. [Letter dated 13 September 1989]

A story about a girl who learns to take charge of herself and which opens to view the inside of contemporary family life, a story of a mystery plot and a mysterious boy (is he real or isn't he?), a story close to fairytale and yet realistic: all this appealed to me. As did the look of the book's pages in the Swedish edition Katarina had given me, with its 150 very short 'chapters', often no more than a few lines long, composed in short, often one-sentence paragraphs. Five of these Katarina had done into English for me—the first three, a few lines of number 36 and all of 109. Only 284 words, but sufficient to create an unusual narrative voice: coolly observant yet sensationally intimate and tuned to an unsentimental lyrical key. Enough also to show me that language itself played as important a role as any of the characters or events. This was the element that finally persuaded me it would be worth publishing a translation.

There now intervened the practical business of negotiating English-language rights, a process not always easy, quick or pleasant but which Eve Lie-Nielsen at Gyldendal Norsk conducted swiftly and with engaging civility. At this point I heard that a professor of epidemiology at the University of Minnesota, David R. Jacobs, had already produced an English text. While holidaying in Norway, Dr Jacobs had come across *Zeppelin* and enjoyed it so much that he had turned it into English in order to share it with his son. Hoping to get his version published, he had sent it to Gyldendal. A good deal of editorial work needed to be done, but, sooner than expected, I could read *Zeppelin*, finding that the book was even better than I'd expected.

And what did I discover? What did the story mean to me when I could read it and before other English-language readers could tell me what it meant to them? What was my *Zeppelin* on first reading? Milan Kundera has explained that his *Book of Laughter and Forgetting* is controlled by a set of key words. It seemed to me that *Zeppelin* was as well. Here is my list.

'Zeppelin', most prominently and obviously. A word handwritten on the kind of shoe we English call 'trainers'. A word that at first confuses (what has an airship to do with this tale?) and later is understood to be a spell, a magic word, a rune, a way into a secret. From the start, then, language is foregrounded, its meaning, its mystery and its music: we are meant to take notice of language, to be conscious of it: written language, language preserved for passage across time and space, language meant for contemplation. This magic word is written by hand on a trainer, itself a word that suggests one meaning the story makes: training in the sense of practising, learning how to do something to the highest possible standard. That it is handwritten on a shoe also points to two more key words:

'Hands, feet'. The first we know of the mysterious intruder is his blue shoes. The first time Nina sees him, a shadowy figure, he waves at her. And when she first finds him hidden in the maple tree in the garden of her family's summerhouse, all she sees is his naked foot. Three chapters later, when handing the trainers up to the unseen boy, his hands brush against hers, the first physical contact, and she knows for sure 'this was no dream'. She breaks into a sweat, as happens when reality overtakes fantasy, feels a pain in her stomach and has to sit down. Hands and feet are all Nina sees of the boy for some time, while bringing him food, until the moment he chases her into the forest, confronts her across a stream, and 'long arms and white fingers' knock her down. Nina screams and holds her hands up to protect herself. But 'Frightened blue eyes peered between her fingers. Gentle eyes. She burst into tears.'

'Let your fingers do the walking,' croons the British advertisement for the *Yellow Pages* telephone directory of business numbers. 'Let your fingers do the talking' would be as apposite to the way hands are put to work in *Zeppelin*, where the symbolic iconography of hands and feet is richly used—the hand as creative maker, as sensor, as that which grasps and holds; the foot as carrier, as mover to and from, as root to the earth. Both are linked to another key word:

'Eyes.' One of the strongest sensations I have in reading *Zeppelin* is of watching. I am watching Nina closely while yet unobserved myself. The mysterious boy is always on the watch. And Nina is a minutely close observer too: of her parents, of the boy in hiding, of the natural world around her—trees, flowers, water, sunlight, moonlight. And as this is a book about language as much as it is about people, places and events, the key words carry pertinent other meanings. Here, the eye by which we see is the 'I' who sees, and the I comes to 'see' what it all means. 'Oh, I see!' we say in English when we mean, 'Now I understand, now I perceive what is meant.' Something else we say, 'At last you've seen the light!' At the end of the book, after the boy says 'You don't even know my name', and Nina replies 'No, but I know who you are', we are left with a particular kind of light: 'Suddenly the moon reached down between the trees. And Nina switched the flashlight off.'

'Light' is the next of the key words, especially the light of the moon, which in this final moment of the story reaches down as if to touch Nina, instantly recalling one of the most tender, sensuous, moving passages in the whole book, the scene in the middle of the night when Nina slips out of the sleeping house and for the first time joins the boy in the tree. By the light of the moon, she lays her index finger on his hand, and with his hand he caresses her hair and delicately draws his finger along the ridge of her nose and over her lips, and she, opening her mouth, tastes on his finger with the tip of her tongue the flavour of maple and silver moon. Then they talk of themselves, of their parents, of what the boy has done and why, during which we read:

The day was for doing things.
The night was for thoughts.
That was how Nina felt.
New thoughts. Other thoughts.
Night thoughts.

The flashlight, which Nina uses more than once, is a modern, 'man'-made implement used when looking for something or finding the way. Its sharply focused, masculine, narrow beam penetrates a small area of the dark. In contrast the moon, ancient, natural, illuminates the night, suffusing it with a soothing light traditionally associated with the imagination, the feminine, the unconscious, and with feelings. By the light of the silvery moon we like to croon in the hope of cuddling soon.

Moon—*la lune*—loony. To be loony, a slang expression dating back to the 1870s, is to be mad. Mad means insane, and also means very angry. There is a good deal of anger in *Zeppelin*: it's a basic element of the plot, for the boy's anger at his parents' lack of attention causes him to run away.

'Attention', then, is a key word, perhaps *the* key word. We need light to see by in order to find our way. We need eyes to see what the light reveals. We need feet to take us where we want to go, and hands to grasp the object of our desire. Most of all, we want attention. When we love someone we attend to them—paying care-full attention is what love is. Attention can become selfish, overweening, which is Nina's oppression, or it can be absent.

'They're always calling me,' Nina said.
'They never call me,' he said.
'They're always asking me what I'm doing and where I am.'
'They never ask me what I'm doing or where I am.'
'I almost never do what I want.'

'I almost always do what I want.'
'I never feel really alone.'
'I always feel alone.'

Nina gives the boy the attention he needs—brings him his shoes so he can walk around, steals food to keep him alive, listens to him, accepts him as he is. The boy gives Nina an understanding of her own predicament and an unselfish purpose, a reason that allows her to achieve the freedom she needs. More than anything, *Zeppelin* is a love story.

It is also a story in which, at the beginning, the boy understands more than the girl who, by the end, understands more than the boy. 'You don't even know my name,' he says on the last page when Nina leaves him hiding in his cave. 'No,' Nina replies, 'but I know who you are.' 'You don't know what zeppelin means either!' he says. 'No,' Nina calls back, 'but I know how it works.' Knowing how the magic works, even though you don't know what it means, knowing that the secret of life lies in paying life itself close loving attention, even though you don't yet know life's meaning, is what the book at its heart is about. Nina has found the way. That's why she can switch the flashlight off and walk by the light of the moon back to her father, who is waiting where she left him on the edge of the forest at the end of the garden path that leads home.

There are dualities throughout the book that suggest more paths in and out of the story:

— the maple tree and the forest;
— Nina's summer home and the other place: the tree, the forest, the land beyond;
— the fenced garden and the unfenced world outside;
— adults and children;
— boy and girl;
— good and bad;
— inside and outside: inside the house, outside in the garden and the forest; in the tree and out of it; the self inside and the other self outside;
— looking at and being looked at;
— the conscious and the unconscious.

*

No matter how simple a good story may seem at first reading, there may be many stories embedded in the primary narrative. How many stories are there in this story?

Most obviously *Zeppelin* is a version of the familiar children's book genre, the holiday adventure. Nina's is an interior adventure. The treasure to be found, the mystery to be solved, the trials to be suffered and overcome are treasures of the spirit, mysteries of consciousness, trials of the mind and the emotions.

To use a term from reception theory, Haugen defamiliarizes the holiday adventure, making strange the too-well-known. He doesn't describe but re-describes.

Then, *Zeppelin* is a family story. Two kinds of family are contrasted in the way that love is expressed, attention paid, truths hidden or told. What are parents' responsibilities towards children? How much, if anything, do children owe their parents? What do adults know that children should not be told? When, as part of growing up, is it necessary and right for children to 'go their own way' in order to 'be themselves', even if this means disobeying or deceiving their parents? Indeed, what does it mean to be a child nowadays?

The story touches each of these questions, investigating without asking them directly. Because they always involve action, character and motive, all stories are by nature moral systems, but some attend to the moral questions, the 'why?' of a character's actions—are 'about' them—whereas others try to ignore them, as for example airport thrillers often do. Literature comes of the one, pastime trash of the other. It would be hard to read *Zeppelin* without addressing the moral questions it poses, for it concerns a turning point in a family's history, and our interest is given to the behaviour of the characters. ('Given to', not 'captured by'. The difference lies in the relationship between author and reader in the text. Writing like Haugen's requires the reader to give willing and wakeful attention to the story. It doesn't attempt to capture the reader's attention with sensationalist or seductive narrative tricks.)

Where does this family holiday drama happen? Setting is often a strong determinant of meaning in a story. Here it is the garden of a summer house and the forest and countryside beyond the garden fence. Our understanding of stories new to us depends on the stories we already know. Perhaps because of my background this element in *Zeppelin* instantly recalls the long English tradition of the enclosed-garden story. Among children's books Frances Hodgson Burnett's *The Secret Garden* and Philippa Pearce's *Tom's Midnight Garden* are two of the best known, but there are many more. In them the English preoccupation with a lost pastoral idyll, the biblical myth of expulsion from Eden for discovering the secrets known only to God the Father, and the maturation psychodramas of our dreams all resonate.

Closed-garden stories are finally about getting out, breaking free, growing up. And usually one character helps another make the escape, sometimes sacrificially dying or remaining prisoner that the other may grow and live. In *Zeppelin* it is the boy who first enables Nina, but at the end it is Nina who has so confidently made the break that she can return to the garden and her waiting father, uninhibitedly as herself, whereas the boy is not only still in the forest but hidden in a (womb-like?) cave, where he will remain, Nina thinks to herself, for a hundred years. He is not yet ready to grow up.

This sequence of moves involving a boy and a girl, a house, a garden, a forest, an escape, and at the end a return to the house, reminds me of another kind of story, the fairytale, and in particular of *Hansel and Gretel*. In that version of the plot, an unloving mother rather than an over-possessive father imprisons the children, but again the boy is the one who, though he begins the rescue, can't carry it through, and it is the girl who 'finds the way' to save them. In both stories an unhappy breakdown between the parents, a dysfunction in properly focused loving attention between parents and children, and an interplay of male and female qualities are the nodal points of the narrative. And both *Hansel and Gretel* and *Zeppelin* conclude with a return home by the protagonists whose relationships have been realigned by a growth in understanding. Those who don't return are either dead, like the stepmother in *Hansel and Gretel*, or are still learning, like the boy in *Zeppelin*, whose understanding and acceptance of the cost of life still need time to mature in the cave-womb behind the fir(fur) forest.

Plenty of straightforward clues signal that the narrator intends us to make this connection.

Zeppelin—
Like something out of a fairy-tale.
Simsalabim, abracadabra and open sesame for treasures hidden in holes and caves.
Fairy-tale treasures.
But *Zeppelin* was there on a real blue trainer.

Zeppelin combines the storytelling contrivances of fairytale and the everyday realities implied by a pubescent boy's distressed trainer. Beginning with the familiar fairytale form, Haugen modulates the narrative into a form that belongs to the great tradition of the literary novel, the character-based moral investigation of everyday life set in the contemporary world.

It is in pubescence that we become seriously self-conscious, begin to delve into the secrets of personality and the motivations of our behaviour. It is then that the subjunctivizing quality of narrative, as Jerome Bruner calls it,* helps our understanding of what it means to be male or female, what it means to be morally courageous, of how grown-up life is a more intricate and subtle matter than the simplistic division of people and experience into good and bad, right and wrong, fair and unfair, either/or.

So, after my first reading of *Zeppelin*, what did I think I'd found? In sum: a novel of contemporary life using the psychologically symbolic resources of fairytale in which a family holiday adventure set in a closed garden with a forest outside is modulated into a psychodrama, a de-identification narrative about the growth from childhood dependency and submission into a first understanding of what it means to be oneself, what it means to attend to another for his or her own sake, accepting the

* 'I have tried to make the case that the function of literature as art is to open us to dilemmas, to the hypothetical, to the range of possible worlds that a text can refer to. I have used the term "to subjunctivize", to render the world less fixed, less banal, more susceptible to recreation. Literature subjunctivizes, makes strange, renders the obvious less so, the unknowable less so as well, matters of value more open to reason and intuition. Literature, in this spirit, is an instrument of freedom, lightness, imagination, and yes, reason. It is our only hope against the long gray night.'

other for what he or she is. The more I thought about it, the more I found myself concentrating on the emergence of Nina from the shadow of, first, her father and then of the boy in the tree. Both male figures are, by the end, stalled, boundaried. Nina makes her father wait at the end of the garden path while she goes through the wild forest to search for the boy. She finds him hiding in a cave. Though he rejects her arrangements for his safe return, she offers continuing help—'I will be here the whole summer, and I thought that maybe we could be friends'—before leaving him in his self-imposed isolation and returning to her waiting father. It is the girl who has taken charge. The men are functioning either at her behest or only because she is keeping them going, in touch with the rest of the world.

Reading *Zeppelin* like that, I realized, is to read it as a modern feminist story: feminist not in the narrow political sense but in the psychological and social senses. My Canadian friend Lissa Paul, a feminist critic of broad sympathies, has shown us how to apply the questions critics ask about a story in order to uncover its gendered stance. I offer a few of the questions here as a game that can be played with *Zeppelin* and with many other children's books.

Who says, and who sees? How often it is the males who speak while Nina listens and watches.

Who orders and who obeys? Always the males at the start, then a shift, towards the end, as Nina gains in moral strength and self-awareness.

Who's on top and why? One example: when Nina first encounters the boy he is 'on top' up in the tree, from which height he commands Nina to help keep him there. By the end Nina stands at the entrance to the cave and, though the text doesn't say so, my own strong impression is that she is looking down at the boy, who is withdrawn, crouching, hunched up inside. Certainly by then Nina is morally and psychologically 'on top'.

Who stays at home and who goes out? Think of those John Ford-style westerns, fairytales about cowboys, in which, at the end, the hero rides off while the wife-lover stands in the doorway of their cave-like cabin watching him go. In *Zeppelin* most of that male-order convention is reversed, so that not only is the girl the hero but she leaves no one behind to struggle on alone while she is adventuring, far removed from domestic responsibility.

Who gains and who loses? Who fights for honour? Who lies and who flees? These questions release the most entertaining revelations of all.

The great Italian fictionalist and critic, Italo Calvino, wrote in his last testament, *Six Memos for the Next Millennium*: 'In the even more congested times that await us, literature must aim at the maximum concentration of poetry and of thought', adding later, 'I would say that today the rule of "Keep It Short" is confirmed even by long novels, the structure of which is accumulative, modular and combinatory'. *Zeppelin* provides a perfect example of Calvino's project, designed with children in mind. There are far too few novels of this kind. Which is part of the crisis I observe besetting literature for children, certainly in the English-speaking nations. The majority of novels and illustrated stories published for young readers nowadays are predictable, look-alike fictions with the unvarying standardized appearance we associate with mass-produced objects. Whereas, as Calvino pointed out:

> In an age when other fantastically speedy, widespread media are triumphing, and running the risk of flattening all communication onto a single, homogeneous surface, the function of literature is communication between things that are different simply because they are different, not blunting but even sharpening the differences between them following the true bent of written language.

Any book that helps us do that for children is exceptionally valuable. *Zeppelin* is one. Its difference from the bulk of stuff published for British youngsters was immediately apparent, even before I could read a word. The 'accumulative, modular and combinatory' structure was made strikingly visible by the arrangement of the text into short, numbered passages, and the short-sentence, concentrated nature of the prose. I was at once reminded of novels like Marguerite Duras' *The Lover* and J.M. Coetzee's *Foe*.

Later, another name was mentioned to me. After a lecture in

Adelaide, South Australia, when I had talked about *Zeppelin*, a high school teacher, Jan Stewart, told me how much she and her pupils had enjoyed the book and that it reminded her of the writing of Norwegian novelist Tarjei Vesaas, particularly *The Ice Palace*. I had to confess that I'd never heard of Vesaas. Jan loaned me her copies of all his work published in English. Here in Elizabeth Rokkan's translation is the opening of part one, chapter four, titled 'The Side of the Road':

> Siss ran home. At once she was struggling blindly with her fear of the dark.
>
> It said: It is I at the sides of the road.
>
> No, no! She thought at random.
>
> I'm coming, it said at the sides of the road.
>
> She ran, knowing there was something at her heels, right behind her.
>
> *Who is it?*
>
> Straight from Unn and into this. Had she not known that the way home would be like this?
>
> She had known, but she had had to go to Unn.
>
> A noise somewhere down in the ice. It ran along the flat expanse and seemed to disappear into a hole. The thickening ice was playing at making mile-long cracks. Siss jumped at the sound.
>
> Out of balance. She had not had anything safe with which to set out on the return journey through the darkness, no firm footsteps striding along the road, as she had when she walked *to* Unn. Thoughtlessly she had started to run, and the damage was done. At once she had been abandoned to the unknown, who walks behind one's back on such evenings.

First published in Norwegian in 1963, in this English translation 1966. Move on thirteen years to 1976 when *Zeppelin* first appeared in Norwegian. Allow for tighter concentration of thought and language, for further paring down of grammar and arrangement of the prose, for a shift of consciousness in the narrator to one overlapping more closely with the central child character, and allow for changes in the use of English between the

1966 translation of Vesaas's Norwegian and the 1991 translation of Haugen's. Then compare the passage above with this from *Zeppelin*, remembering that Siss and Nina are about the same age:

> Nina stared at the path which curved enticingly under the dark spruce trees.
>
> The path went on and on.
>
> She stood still.
>
> All at once she felt it.
>
> Someone was looking at her.
>
> The *stare* glided over her back and tickled her neck. Her scalp itched.
>
> Slowly she turned round.
>
> No one. Nothing.
>
> But someone was looking at her. She tried to meet the *stare*, but where should she look?
>
> She let her eyes sweep over the garden.
>
> She tried to see through the bushes.
>
> She tried to peer through the foliage.
>
> Come out! she thought, but no one came.
>
> She stood and waited. With her back to the fence. To the path. To the woods. To the darkness under the trees.
>
> It was as if the day grew dark and the light turned pale and the wind grew stronger and the birds shrieked.
>
> Suddenly she knew that something big and black was creeping along the path.

There is a family likeness, a similarity in the cast of mind and the structuring of language. Certainly, having read both books one after the other, I was struck by the shared atmosphere, not just of the story but of setting and attitude to the tale. It isn't at all English, or American or Australian. I found myself wondering how influential Vesaas was, how likely it was that he stood at Haugen's shoulder in the way that writers sometimes feel their formative predecessors watching over them and guiding their hand. And is a genetic link between *The Ice Palace* and *Zeppelin* commonly recognized by Norwegian readers? Roger G. Popperwell, Lecturer in Norwegian at the University of Cambridge, assessing Vesaas in the *Penguin Companion to Literature*, notices 'the highly sensitive but quiet awareness of the psychological significance of the minutiae of experience, sense impressions and silence, which is characteristic of his work', the 'tightly packed, symbolic style' of his books published in the 1940s, which inaugurate a new period that includes 'more concrete' novels like *The Ice Palace* and remarks finally on 'his qualities as a lyricist and psychologist'. It seems to me that all this could be said about Tormod Haugen.

The narrative techniques of *Zeppelin* remind me of another form: screenplay for film and television. The story even looks like a film script, with its sequence of numbered shots, a narrative that gives clear angles of sight and indications of action, includes lines of dialogue without suggesting how they are to be spoken, and brief, precise notations of setting, design, lighting. There is also that aspect of life which screenplay never deals with very well and which is the great glory of the novel: the drama of interior life, the life of the mind and spirit. But in *Zeppelin* even this is handled so that a good actor and director could find ways of suggesting what is going on in a character but not being said. So strongly is screenplay present in the book that I'd be willing to bet that Haugen is a keen student of film.*

The English-language edition of *Zeppelin* was published in Britain and Australia in 1991 and in the USA in 1994. In Britain, the critical reception was barely noticeable, by which I mean there were very few reviews and no mentions on tv or radio. The most appreciative comment appeared in Margery Fisher's thirty-year-old, one-woman enterprise, the review journal *Growing Point*. For her, the novel was a sociological study of family life:

> There is an element of childhood adventure in *Zeppelin* as Nina retrieves a lost trainer for the oddly named boy and climbs into his refuge to hear more about his indifferent parents and his plans for an active protest against their neglect; but she acts still more decisively when she speaks out for all children forced to

* After delivering this celebration, I learned that Haugen is indeed a passionate film buff.

> take a hard look at their elders and betters. From Norway, cast in the form of short paragraphs indicating changes of scene or of actors leading to longer scenes in house or garden, the story is told in a laconic, detached style so that the author never intrudes on the two young people who carry the mood and tone of a searching view of family life in our times. (*Growing Point*, July 1991, page 5549)

Eva Walber ended a fourteen-line review in the *Eastern Daily Press*, 14 March 1991: 'A deeply sensitive exploration of loyalty, honesty and problems with parents, the style trembles with taut intensity.' Sarah Balderson, a secondary school teacher writing in the Spring 1992 *Essex Review*, thought the novel

> rather strange and it is difficult to say whether I enjoyed it or not. [. . .] There is a fairytale quality about the book: language and plot alike. [. . .] A strong point was the simple layout which made the book very accessible. Also, the vocabulary was straightforward, just as it would be from a child's viewpoint. The book could be read on a very simple level but the messages concerning growing up and parental conflict were there and would be apparent to the older reader. [. . .] It's worth a read!

In the years since publication the paperback publishers, essential these days to the commercial success of any book, have rejected it as a 'literary' book 'not sufficiently saleable to the mass market'. And that was about it where Britain was concerned.

In Australia, where there are more outlets for children's book reviews than there are now in Britain, reaction was livelier. Writing in *Magpies* for July 1991 Joan Zahnleiter, an experienced and widely read librarian, noted that

> this psychological mystery adventure story has, in fact, many layers of meaning. It has the reader hurtling down its short lines in pursuit of the few clues upon which the adults in the story manage to build a fantasy that terrifies them. For Nina and the nameless boy in the blue gym shoes, what transpires over those few summer days and nights is, in fact, a rite of passage. They pass from being dependent children to young people who want

a say in how their lives are run. [. . .] For the young people there is fantasy of another kind revealed in Nina's nocturnal journey through the woods, in which she uses the password 'Zeppelin' to thwart the forces of evil which try to waylay her.

In the other of Australia's two major children's books review magazines, *Reading Time* (vol. 35, no. 3), the reviewer wrote:

> The story is sometimes realistic, sometimes surreal, and it raises several central issues for children approaching the end of childhood and the beginning of adolescence. There is the growing awareness that parents' views of the world are not always accurate, sensible or even comprehensible, there is the inner sense of a developing personal autonomy and sensuality. Ultimately, and perhaps most interestingly, there are no easy answers given at the end of this book. Though this commentary might make the novel seem a moral tale, it is not. It is mostly a charming, poetic and suspenseful tale that grapples with real emotions.

Published in the USA in 1994 under the title *Keeping Secrets*, the reaction has been as mixed as it was in Britain and not much greater in volume. '[T]he book has an unusual format,' reported the influential *Publishers Weekly*, 'with poetic sentences arranged in numbered stanzas, and it comes off a little mannered at first. But once the novelty wears off, the structure provides a serious framework for the dreamy yet evocative text.' Sharon Korbeck, writing in the equally influential *School Library Journal*, decided that 'The writing becomes cleaner and more fluid toward the end of the book, when more of the plot becomes evident. But the meaning and power of the word 'zeppelin' is never explained. The confusing sentence structure and lack of much suspense detract from [his] novel, and readers are sure to be left wondering about the significance of it all. It doesn't contain enough fantasy to qualify on that level, and its realism is too obscure.'

A view echoed in *The Bulletin of the Centre for Children's Books*: 'Although the characterization is abstracted, delineating the children and parents only in terms of each other, there's enough of an emotional tug that readers may forgive the shortchanged treatment.' On the other hand, *Kirkus Review*, which covers books in general, not only children's books, and is noted for its literary acumen and no-nonsense judgements, summed up its opinion thus: 'Broken into 150 fragments and written in a spare poetic style, the story gradually emerges from a dreamy glancing-off narrative while Nina floats from shadowy awareness to a steadier grasp of the world and herself.'

In 1995 HarperCollins (US) decided *Keeping Secrets* hadn't sold well enough to justify its continued existence, remaindered the unsold stock and put their edition out of print.

Together these notices provide material for a useful study of the assumptions made by reviewers of children's fiction about the nature of children, the nature of reading, and the reviewer's role as guide and commentator.

So much for adults with a public voice. What about young readers themselves? I have a twenty-five-minute videotape and three letters from a group of ten girls, thirteen-year-old pupils at the Wilderness School in Adelaide, South Australia. It was their English teacher, Jan Stewart, who drew my attention to the likeness between Vesaas and Haugen. I asked Jan if any of her pupils were reading *Zeppelin* and whether they would let me know what they thought of it. Here is a summary of their videotaped comments:

—All the girls liked the book. *Zeppelin* was, they say—and I'm gathering key phrases together—'original', especially in 'the way it was set out and the style', 'it was unusual' in the 'different styles of writing'. At first, they agree, it seemed 'strange' but then, after they'd read it for a while, began to seem 'normal'.

—It was about 'the two sides of Nina', the good and bad, and two kinds of parents, one 'restrictive', one 'unrestrictive'.

—It was about secrets Nina had and kept.

—That Nina was an only child made a difference. Parents of only children behave differently from those with larger families.

—What Nina wants to be is herself.

—They remark on and all liked the day/night, good/bad dual nature of the story.

—The boy helps Nina 'break out' and start to become herself. But, one girl suggested, perhaps the boy wasn't real, only imaginary. The shoes were there, but perhaps Nina invented the boy to go with them. [Not a view generally accepted.]

—Picking up the shoes was 'the first step' [no one reacted to the pun] Nina takes to 'breaking out', 'becoming herself'.

—The story is 'like a fairytale at the end', 'and there's a passage that says it is'.

—They liked the ending, even though at first some of them had felt uneasy about it (what happened to the boy, they wondered). 'But that is how it had to be.'

—The father daring 'to stand there alone' [p. 124] at the end: 'Daring to do what? To leave each other . . . become separate . . . not a family any more in the way they had been before.'

—You must 'become your own person'.

What were the differences they'd noticed between this book and others?

—The short chapters. 'They were like poems in themselves.' They were easy to read and kept you going, but especially at the beginning they were poem-like and included what one of the girls calls 'key words'. Each chapter, one girl suggests, is 'an idea-group'. Another says that every chapter represents a 'vision, like a snapshot'.

—They were not used to such a way of telling a story, but soon got used to it and then liked it.

—They also liked it that there was 'no description' of the characters.

I have heard similarly thoughtful comments from students in Britain, some as young as nine, some as old as undergraduates training to be teachers. One reaction is common to them all: *Zeppelin* is not the kind of book that many people choose to read for themselves. It needs an intermediary. My own experience is that the best thing to do is say very little about the story but read aloud chapters 17 to 21, the passages in which Nina and her parents arrive at the summer holiday house, find there has been an intruder, and discover the blue trainers. That's enough to raise interest and show how the narrative works. It is the kind of book about which there is little to be said before reading it and a great deal afterwards.

Which brings me back to an earlier point, about making value judgements and taking responsibility for other people's reading. It is inescapable that learner-readers—in fact, all of us all the time—depend on someone else's choice of books before they can choose for themselves. Judgements about value, about the importance of introducing young readers to this book rather than that and to introduce it now rather than later, are never easy to make, and are fraught with educational, political and moral problems. Making such judgements should not be done by individual teachers and librarians on their own. Those of us who accept the responsibility should talk among ourselves, discovering how best to bring this book to young readers. The list—the canon—will change constantly. That's right, and inevitable. What matters is how the changes come to be made: whose voices are heard, how opinions are expressed, which questions need to be asked. As a student teacher I would never have thought to ask the kinds of feminist questions posed earlier. Now that I've been taught to ask them by a friendly colleague, my view of some children's books has changed. To put it in the words of Wayne C. Booth in *The Company We Keep: An Ethics of Fiction*: 'The goal is not to pack into our traveling bag only the best that has been thought and said but to find forms of critical talk that will improve the range or depth or precision of our appreciations [...] a kind of conversation that might *get somewhere*—not just a sharing of subjective opinions but a way of learning from one another.'

This is an urgent task. We professionals need to know how to talk better among ourselves, and we need to know how to help students talk better about their reading. My own reading of *Zeppelin* suggests that it occupies a rare place in current children's literature. A few lines from early in the book sum it up.

Best to be careful.
Zeppelin—just a little thought.
The word glowed.
Nina closed her eyes and let it sink into her.
How odd—
It was as if the word fell into place inside her.

The Future of the Book

In the late 1980s I watched a tv interview with Bill Gates, head of Microsoft. This is the gist of what he said. In twenty-five years or so eighty per cent of the books now published will have disappeared, their function taken over by electronic forms of communication. Libraries and bookshops will be very different places. In the same period of time, a revolution will take place in both hardware and the software that will be as great as the revolution we have experienced in the fifty years or so since the Second World War. 'It is a revolution so great,' he said to the interviewer, 'it is beyond your imagination.'

For a while I was worried. I am a dyed-in-the-word book person. Until the end of my days, and while my faculties allow, I shall be a reader and writer of books-as-we-know-them. Then the thought occurred: If eighty per cent of books disappear, this means twenty per cent will still remain. Gates had said nothing about these. Which ones will remain, and why? If I am to go on reading and writing, if I am to go on living with confidence as a book person, I need to know.

What is there that we can *know* about the speciality of the Book? What *is* a book? No one in the whole of my life as a learner and a teacher has ever asked me for a definition or considered it necessary to be explicit about the object itself. This is not surprising. While a form of communication is dominant, we take it for granted. (Think of television, as a medium of communication now—has anyone ever defined it for you or have you felt the need to define it for yourself?) Only when it is under threat or has been overtaken in predominance by another form do we begin to wonder why, and whether it is necessary. The Book is in exactly that position now.

Arriving at a workable definition began for me one day when

tutoring a group of undergraduate teachers-in-training. By the time we had finished we knew that the Book did indeed possess a unique nature. And although the standard dictionary definitions had been of some help, we knew they had omitted the essence, the feature which supplies a unique value of the Book.

We reminded ourselves that a definition must include only the features essential to the object in question, without qualifying conditionals. And so we began:

A book is

One of the fundamental features we agreed upon very quickly is that a book is composed of a number pages. A single page, a single leaf of paper doesn't make a book. Nor does a single leaf folded into, say, four or six pages. Nor do any number, no matter how many, of loose pages. Necessarily, a book contains more than a few pages, and the pages must belong together in some kind of related sequence that makes a whole. Thus:

A book is a sequence of pages

And of course, we readily agreed, books communicate something. A gathering of blank pages do not make a book, unless an adjective indicates a conditional purpose—'drawing book', 'note book', 'account book'. These are incipient books. They are waiting for someone to inscribe communicating signs on to their blank surfaces. They are would-be but not-yet books.

Furthermore, these signs—letters, words, figures, diagrams, maps, musical notations, drawings of artistic or technical kinds, mathematical and scientific formulae, architectural plans, on and on—can be inscribed onto blank pages in many ways: by hand with pencil, ink and brush, by traditional mechanical printing methods, and nowadays by electronic equipment. The time is not far off when pages can be made not from paper but from synthetic material capable of displaying electronically delivered signs, and yet the pages will be presented as a book or, as is already available, as an electronic 'reader'—a book-like machine with a screen rather than separate pages, but presenting the text page-by-page as in a traditional book. So we cannot simply say that books are (or will be) those printed in the way that has long been familiar. Signs may appear on a page by various means. It doesn't matter how they get there so long as the means of delivery conforms to the other features required by the definition of the Book. Thus we have a sequence of pages:

on which appear

The signs themselves also communicate meanings of various kinds. We read books because they 'make sense' not just of one kind but of many different kinds, and not in one way only but in different ways. Our definition needed a phrase that would cover all these, including the possibility that some of the signs might be entirely abstract and without conventional commonplace meaning—the book equivalent of abstract paintings. Strictly speaking, these should not be called 'signs' because the word is associated with shapes that have an agreed meaning, whereas unconventional, non-specific abstract shapes invite new meaning to be made by the reader or viewer. We found this the hardest part of the definition to solve. The phrase we finally agreed on is not elegant, and includes a metaphor taken from the old way of inscription, for to be literal, all-inclusive and succinct was not otherwise possible. So, a sequence of pages on which appear

meaning-communicating marks

At this point we realized that it is possible to have a gathering of loose pages on which there are communicating marks, with the pages numbered to indicate a sequence, yet still this would not constitute a book. To be a book, we felt, the pages should be held together unalterably.* Therefore, a book is a sequence of pages on which appear meaning-communicating marks,

all of which are bound together.

* A few books which are not bound, such as *The Unfortunates*, a novel by B. S. Johnson, which is presented as loose pages contained in a box, provide examples that prove the rule by being deliberate rare exceptions.

For a while we thought this was a complete definition. We thought the binding was required only to keep the pages together so that none would be lost or shuffled into a wrong order. Then we noticed the wording: that all the elements—all the meaning-communicating marks as well as the pages—are bound together. And we began to realize that binding everything together has a deeper significance than merely the prevention of loss or misplacing of pages.

This thought prompted the question, Who decides that everything shall be bound together in a particular order, not merely to prevent accidental loss or disturbance, but so that nothing can be deliberately rearranged? The answer is, the person who is attempting to communicate with us, the person 'composing' the book: the author.

It is the writer of the communication, the composer of the text, the author, who chooses the signs and arranges the sequence of the pages. And the main reason for binding the book is to make sure that the author's sequence is preserved and not interfered with.

We understood at once that we had identified not only another essential feature of a book, but the one that turns out to be the defining feature of all—the one that makes sense of all the others and on which they depend, the one that tells us everything about the difference between the Book and every other form of communication. In key words, a book is bound

in an authorized order.

Only when we had tested it every which way could we be sure we had achieved a satisfactory definition, and after much further thought about it and discussion of it with many others, it still seems to me to be valid.

A book is
a sequence of pages
on which appear meaning-communicating marks,
all of which are bound together
in an authorized order.

Two kinds of Authority

N.B. In order to deal with the problem of gendered pronouns, in what follows I use the pronoun 'she' when referring to the author and 'he' when referring to the reader or user of a book.

Author. Authorization. Authority. At once this definition indicates one of two kinds of authority entailed in a book.

The first and most obvious is the primary authority of the writer who arranged the words on the page, arranged the pages in a sequence, and indicated her intention by binding the pages together. To interfere with this—to rearrange or remove any of the pages, or to remove or change the words—is a violation. By its nature and purpose, a book requires those who use it to exercise particular responsibilities, one of which is that the integrity of the author's composition shall be respected, whatever the user may think about it.

The other authority, less obvious at first, but clear as soon as we begin to use a book, is the co-equal authority of the user/reader. He may do as he pleases with the text, and with the book itself, for who can prevent him? He can read it backwards, dip and skip, can read for a while and break off for a while, can read some parts and never read the rest. If he wants to, the reader can use a book as a doorstop or—so long as he owns the copy—tear the pages out and use them to wrap up his rubbish or to light a fire. In this sense, as we have often been told, the reader is in charge and the author is powerless.

But the responsible reader honours the unwritten contract that requires him to respect what the author has made and not tamper with it. He will sample the book in order to decide whether or not it is something he wants to read, something worth his time. When his sampling or first quick reading proves the text is exceptionally worthwhile, he respects what the author has made and attends to the text *as a whole and in the order of its bound-together sequence*. Indeed, with the best and greatest texts, rereading of the whole, the boring passages as well as those that are immediately appealing, is essential.

Looked at from the reader's point of view, it is clear that, just as readers have a responsibility to authors, so authors have a responsibility to readers. Authors must respect readers by giving the best of themselves to their work—the totality of their skill, knowledge, experience, understanding, care, and, above all, their command of language.

This mutual respect and bipartite authority are sited not in author and reader as persons but in the Book. The Book is the source of their pleasure. It is the Book, the making of it and the reading of it, which creates their authority. It is because of the Book that communication occurs. The Book is the location and the focus of their respect and attention. It is the book itself which authorizes them.

Responsible writers and responsible readers know this. They talk of how a book absorbs them, of how they can lose themselves in it, of how it takes them over, lives in them, changes them (however minutely each time), how it adds to their experience, knowledge, development, personality. They value most those books that transcend their ability to use language, present ideas, inquire into human behaviour. The books that matter most to authors and readers are those that speak to them and speak for them, expressing better than they can themselves that which they already know and that which they are glad to learn.

The Book and other media

All of which may be the case, but is it any the less so of, say, a film or a stage play or a tv or radio programme or a text on the internet? Are there differences between the Book and all other forms of communication? There are.

One key difference is that, in other forms of communication, various interpreters come between the writer and the audience. In film, for example, there are a producer, a director, the actors, set and costume designers, a music director, sound and lighting designers, and an editor. Every one of them has a view—an interpretation—of the text's meaning. Usually of course, it is the producer's or director's interpretation that predominates. And everything in the making of the film is done to present that interpretation to the audience. This is also true of plays on stage, tv and radio (and indeed of every kind of broadcast programme, including the 'news'). Even when a text is read aloud the same thing is happening: the reader-aloud is interpreting the text for us. One reader-aloud can make a text funny and another make the same text sad or poignant. Even the simplest fact, that we must listen to the words spoken at the speed the performer chooses to read them, interprets their meaning. Of course, we must judge for ourselves whether the interpretation is one we can accept or agree with. But the point is that in all these forms of communication we are recipients of other people's interpretations.

But when we read a book for ourselves we are on our own. We are the most in charge of the interpretation—the making of sense—that we ever can be. We must be our own producer, director, actors, light and sound designers, music director and editor; not least, we must be our own literary critic. Which is why reading a book is the most difficult, the most testing form of communication. We should never underestimate the skill and experience involved. The pleasure is more hard-won than the pleasure of listening to radio or watching a film or tv programme. But nothing else provides the same rewards.

In writing and reading a book responsibility is left completely to the individual person without imposition by institutional authority. This is embedded in the nature of the Book, which is why totalitarians of every stripe—political, religious, economic and educational—are bothered by books, why they try to control their publication and distribution, even to the point of banning and burning them.

The Book is in fact the very icon of the civilization to which we belong, the Greco-Hebraic-Christian tradition, which combines the idea of the unique individual with the idea of the community. In this culture, individuals are seen as having an integrity that must not be violated—murder and rape, torture and assault, for example, are wrong. Individuals are accorded rights. At the same time, they are understood to be citizens of a collective, with responsibilities and duties to the society that grants and protects those rights. Which means that the responsibilities are mutual, for individual and society alike.

Books are individual objects, but similar in kind, just as human beings are individuals and yet are like each other in kind. Books have an integrity which must not be abused—ripping out pages, changing words on the pages, 'murdering' the book by burning it or tearing it up in order to annihilate it, are wrong. But equally, all books belong to a family we call a genre or form, and a community we call a library. They are in themselves the focus of responsibilities to be exercised by whoever makes and uses them.

Not only is the Book an icon of our civilization, I would argue that it is one of the elements that helped create it. The dual authority of the Book is the dual authority embedded in our civilisation, in our ways of thought and in our behaviour.

In other words, the Book enshrines integrity.

However, in electronic communication—the form that seems to be taking over and which some people say will completely replace the Book—there is no integrity either in the print itself or the means by which it is delivered. For example, we now know that you cannot trust the accuracy of anything that comes to you by electronic means, least of all anything that comes to you through the internet. No user knows for certain who put the message there, or whether it was transcribed accurately. In most cases it is not possible to establish easily if at all who is responsible for it, whereas a book provides information, certain details of which are required by law, about the writer, the publisher, the printer, dates of production, and the holder of the copyright, all of whom can be held to account.

In sum: in no other form of verbal communication, in no other art than that we call literature, is the communicator as much in command of the medium as when composing a book; in no other is the recipient as much in control of the medium as a reader is when reading a book; in no other is the mind of the recipient in such direct and intimate touch with the mind of the communicator; in no other is there as much left for the recipient to do in the making of the experience as there is for a reader; in no other is it as possible to achieve such a density, such subtlety, such inexhaustible ambiguity, such multiplicity of meanings as in a book. And the mystery of this (to some degree it is inexplicable) is not in the words—a book-load of print-like words can be beamed at you from a computer screen without having the same effect—the mystery is not in the words but on the page.

What is the mystery of the page? Young children, when they are learning to read, instinctively demonstrate one aspect of it. They hug books to them and lick and paw at the pages. One reason a book and its pages are so important is that they are tactile. The Book, an object made of pages, is designed for holding in the hand; the binding is designed so that pages can be easily turned and held open. Indeed, a book when held is like an extension of the hand, the pages like extra fingers. The physicality of book reading, the visceral nature of it, its appeal to our fingers as well as to our eyes, is fundamental to the experience of reading, which means that it is also fundamental to the meaning we make out of what we read.

The medium used to present a text considerably influences our understanding of, our attitude to, our judgements about the text. We read a broadsheet newspaper differently from a book; we read a hand-written message on a single sheet of paper differently from a printed brochure; we read a child's exercise book differently from a bound monograph. And we read texts presented on computer screen differently from the same text presented in a book.

In fact this is such a deeply influential matter that we read a text presented in one format of book differently from the same text presented in another format. For example, as a school librarian I once conducted an experiment. I placed on the shelves hardback copies of a youth novel and waited to see what would happen. The book was rarely taken out. After three months, I replaced the hardback copies with paperback copies of the same book. These were often borrowed. I then placed hardback copies mixed in with paperback copies. The hardback copies were rarely borrowed, the paperback copies often were. When I discussed the experiment with a group of readers, they assured me that the hardback copies were 'not as interesting', the story, they said, was 'not as good' when read in hardback.

Another example. I first read James Joyce's *Ulysses* in the first Bodley Head edition, which had a square format rather too large for comfort, with a long reading line that tired the eye. It seemed a very cerebral novel, intellectually demanding, and 'tough'.

Years later I read it again in a new Bodley Head edition, this time presented as a much smaller, almost paperback-sized volume, rather like a fat bible, with narrow lines of print. This time the text seemed to me not only easier to read but much more lyrical and emotional in effect. I don't think I felt this difference only because I was reading the book for a third or fourth time but because it was in a more agreeable format. And I know, as most people say they know, the huge difference there is between reading a text on a screen and reading the same text printed out on a sheet of paper. (A small but important example: Most writers and editors I talk to tell me they find it harder to proof read accurately when the text is on a screen; they only catch all the errors when the text is printed out. Of course, this may be conditioned. We are still more used to dealing with paper-printed texts than with screened texts. Maybe many years from now people will proofread on screen comfortably and accurately. But it is not the case at the moment.)

The experience of reading a story or a poem on book pages is noticeably different from reading it on a screen. For me, screened texts are not only much less pleasurable to read but my focus of attention is less concentrated. I am less patient with them, take less in, and am less aware of the play of meaning(s), probably because the visceral, emotional and intellectual link in human nature between the actively involved hand and the eye is denied when reading screened texts. (It is noticeable how children especially, but adults too, tend to touch the screen with a finger when they are telling you about screened texts. They instinctive try to re-establish the hand-eye link because it is so helpful when trying to explain something that's difficult.)

The ways in which hand and eye work together, what each does, determines the nature of the experience, the pleasure we enjoy and, where reading is concerned, not just the meaning of the texts but the meaning of the whole event: of the look and feel, even the smell, of a book, of selecting what to read, of visiting the text through the medium of the stable, unchangeable page, of considering what we've read and rereading in order to reconsider and newly experience the unchanged text.

In earlier times when the Book was dominant the visceral nature of book reading was taken for granted. Nowadays, when electronic texts do not possess the integrity of separate pages, the physical aspect of the book makes it special and different, and needs to be reflected upon—not just because it affects the reader's understanding but because it affects the writer as well. Writing for a book page is different from writing for electronic display. The developing styles of email and text messaging are clear and simple cases in point. The boundaries are different. The grouping and bordering of lines of words are different. The way in a book the turnover of a page can be used in the making of meaning and the guidance of interpretation is obliterated by electronic display. And users of a screen text can alter the arrangement of the words at the touch of a button. The stable nature, the vital integrity of the page is lost.

A final key difference. Electronic forms of communication share one basic element that is the very opposite of books. They invite interference. They are designed both in their hardware and their software so that the user can change and manipulate the text easily and expects to do so. The word 'interactive' has been taken over by electronic communicators as their own in order to name an attractive aspect of their means of exchange.

The Book possesses other qualities that make it profoundly different from every other medium. These have been rehearsed often enough. The user-friendliness of a book and of book print. The way pages of book print—their shape and size, the texture and even the colour of the paper—have been refined over hundreds of years to a format and appearance that exactly fit the human hand, so that the object is a pleasure to hold and look at, and suits the human eye and what it can comfortably take in as it views the print.

Anyone who has spent any length of time working on a word-processor while also using books, as I am at this minute, will know how different it is looking at the words on the screen and looking at the same words on a book page. I know which I prefer and find most engaging and easiest to deal with as a reader. As a writer, of course, the advantages of preparing a text on a computer are much greater than when doing so on paper. Yet still I write my novels with a pencil on paper before redrafting them on screen, because the nature of composing a narrative by hand on paper is so completely different from typing on to a screen.

A Parallel History

There is a parallel history that can help us when thinking about the future of the Book. In the mid-nineteenth century, photography emerged as a new form of visual record. Lewis Carroll was among those who took it up and made superb images using it. Ever since the year dot, people had drawn and painted images as the only way of recording visual experience—how they and their relatives looked, important events, landscape, scientific experiments. Now photography could record all these more easily. There were pundits who said that painting was now finished, dead. But there were others who questioned that prophecy and set about analysing in theory and practice what it is about paint and painting that makes it unlike every other form of visual communication, especially different from photography, and whether there is something unique about it that is essential to human life.

At about the same time, another technical development took place. Prepared oil paint contained in small tubes became available. For the first time it was possible to paint easily in the open air and to capture the quickly changing colours of the landscape almost as it was happening before the artist's eyes. No need for the time-consuming, skilled work of grinding and preparing one's own colours in the closed environment of the artist's studio.

The result of theory, practice and this lucky, timely technical development was the emergence of impressionism, and after it of post-impressionism, cubism, and all the other movements and modes of painting that belong to the greatest flourishing of painting since the Renaissance. Released from the need to make representational, documentary images and to cover everything else in the visual field, artists could concentrate on the nature of paint itself and of painting as an art form, and find out new ways of looking at and presenting the world in paintings. So vital to their own lives do large numbers of people from all walks of life find this form of human engagement with the world around them that galleries which display paintings from all periods are vigorously attended, to the extent that in recent years they have been some of the most visited and loved places in every city. There have never been so many people painting, so many offering their work for sale, so many galleries open to the public.

So much, then, for a dead art! My contention is that as we move into the new millennium and what some have called 'the post-industrial era of technology', with the accompanying pronouncements of the death of the book, we book-loving people will have to perform a similar act of rediscovery of literature-in-print as lovers of painting did for their art form. And the best way to do this will be not by devising theories but by thoughtful practice: by writers and readers working it out together through their experience of writing and reading books that exploit the difference of the book form. The more I try to explore that work myself, the more sure I become that the result could be the same for book-literature as it was in painting: a great new flourishing just when it looks as though the form is finished.

As Guglielmo Cavallo and Roger Chartier demonstrate in *A History of Reading in the West*, every evolutionary development in the technology and presentation of texts changes reading practices. As happened, for example, in the change from stone to papyrus, papyrus to vellum and vellum to paper, from roll to codex, from manuscript to machine printing. Every major development in the technology has been followed by an evolutionary growth in writing and reading. When, for example, writers changed from using pens to typewriters the novel and poetry changed too. And there are those who suggest that the increasing number of very long novels being produced today has more to do with the ease with which writers can write and rewrite on screen and the time it saves, leaving more time to write more text, than it has to do with readers' preference for long novels. As D.F. McKenzie puts it in *Bibliography and the Sociology of Texts*, 'New readers . . . make new texts, and . . . their new meanings are a function of their new forms.' There is every reason why a similar sea change should happen again as it has in the past as a result of current developments in the technology of texts.

The Book exists only for print and for reading. That is its purpose. Every form of electronic 'print' (for it is not print at all) is part of something else. E-texts are only part of equipment that has other uses, equipment designed for manipulating electronic pulses.

We need what the Book encourages: time to dwell on the settled quiet page and the reader's most efficient control of the writing within the authorized sequence. Because we need this, the Book is far from finished and is entering an era when it is more necessary than ever.

When we read a book, we have in our hands a vision composed (in English) of twenty-six abstract signs ordered into horizontal lines and separated by spaces and a few other abstract marks that indicate how to orchestrate the pages in the theatre of our own imagination, where we interpret the vision for ourselves, taking it at the pace we prefer, flicking back and forth and skipping and stopping and starting when we feel like it. It is ours in a way nothing else can be. No one comes between the consciousness that composed the vision and our own.

Literature is written language communicating one consciousness as intimately and directly as possible with the consciousness of 'the other': the reader. As we read we feel strongly and are affected by the vision we inhabit and that inhabits us. Yet, mysteriously at the same time we can stand back and consider what is happening to us and why. We take part in the event—indeed, we are the event—but we are outside it too, looking on.

The audience for a book is one. But so perfect is the design for its purpose that the singular book can easily be reproduced as many times as is required. Whether or not vast numbers of people want to own copies has nothing to do with the Book's reasons for being. To judge success by large-quantity sales is to confuse a book's easy reproducibility for its main purpose.

Mass production is not the main purpose of the Book. Rather a book is intended as a means of printing messages in a stable and convenient physical form—that is, to preserve an authorized communication.

If it is written language that matters, we need the Book, because the Book is the home where written language lives and where readers live with written language. Whether Bill Gates's twenty percent or some other figure turns out to be accurate doesn't matter. What matters is that the Book will flourish at last as an unfettered art form. Literature is made of authorized language meant for reader-controlled contemplation. That is the essence of the thing, the difference of the Book from all else. And its future is abundant.

REFERENCES & BOOKS CONSULTED

The number before an entry refers to the page in *Reading Talk* on which the book is quoted. Where a book is quoted from several times, the references are given at the end of the entry, with the *Reading Talk* page indicated first, in roman, and the quoted page indicated second, in italic.

69 Thomas Arnold, *Fragment on the Church*, quoted in Trevor, page 40

88 Correlli Barnett, *The Collapse of British Power* (1972), quoted in P.J. Rich, *Elixir of Empire: The English Public Schools, Ritualism, Freemasonry and Imperialism*), London: Regency Press, second edition 1993, page 125

Willis Barnstone, *The Poetics of Translation: History, Theory, Practice*, New Haven: Yale University Press, 1993

120-1 Anthea Bell, 'Translator's Notebook: Delicate Matters', *Signal* 49, January 1986, pages 17, 20

114 Anthea Bell, 'Translator's Notebook: The Naming of Names', *Signal* 46, January 1985, page 4

122 Walter Benjamin, 'The Task of the Translator', *Illuminations* (1955), edited by Hannah Arendt, translated by Harry Zohn, London: Fontana/Collins, 1973, page 79

John Berger, *Keeping a Rendezvous*, London: Granta Books, 1992

156 Wayne C. Booth, *The Company We Keep: An Ethics of Fiction*, Berkeley: University of California Press, 1988, pages 113, 421

114 Dorothy Briley, 'Publishing Translations for Children', *Children's Book Council Newsletter*, New York, 1987

122 Robert Browning, quoted in Barnstone, 37

146 Jerome Bruner, *Actual Minds, Possible Worlds*, Cambridge MA: Harvard University Press, 1986, page 159

148 Italo Calvino, *Six Memos for the Next Millennium*, Cambridge MA: Harvard University Press, 1988, pages 51, 120, 45

Guglielmo Cavallo & Roger Chartier, *A History of Reading in the West*, translated by Lydia G. Cochrane, Cambridge: Polity Press, 1999

35 Samuel L. Clemens (Mark Twain), *The Adventures of Huckleberry Finn*, with an introduction by T.S. Eliot (1950), London: Cresset Press, page vii

121 Erasmus, preface to his New Testament, quoted in Barnstone, page 52

77 F.W. Farrar, Preface to *Eric, or Little by Little*, 24th edition, 1889, quoted in Quigly, page 70

115-6 Klaus Flugge, *The Times Educational Supplement*, 31 March 1991

Anne Frank, *The Diary of Anne Frank* (1947), translated from the Dutch by B.M. Mooyaart-Doubleday, foreword by Storm Jameson. First published by Pan Books, 1954. London: Pan Horizons, 1989. The quoted lines on page 10 appear on pages 215-6 of this edition; the line quoted on page 15 appears on page 14.

Anne Frank, *The Diary of a Young Girl: The Definitive Edition*, edited by Otto H. Frank & Mirjam Pressler, translated by Susan Massotty (Viking, 1997) copyright © The Anne Frank-Fonds, Basle Switzerland, 1991. English translation copyright © Doubleday a division of Bantam Doubleday Dell Publishing Group Inc., 1995. Except where noted above, lines quoted throughout the article come from the Puffin Books edition, 1997. The extracted quotes on pages 16, 17, 20, 21 and 23 appear on pages 146, 160, 330, 248 and 326-7 of this edition.

21-2 Miep Gies with Alison Leslie Gold, *Anne Frank Remembered: The Story of the Woman Who Helped to Hide the Frank Family*, Simon & Schuster, Touchstone edition, 1988, pages 186-7

47 Virginia Hamilton, *The People Could Fly: American Black Folktales*, Alfred A. Knopf, 1985, page 5

Tormod Haugen, *Zeppelin*, Woodchester: Turton & Chambers, 1991

37, 44 Ernest Hemingway, in Larry Phillips, editor, *Ernest Hemingway on Writing*, London: Granada, 1985, page 93

68-9 Thomas Hughes, *Tom Brown's Schooldays* (1857), London: Dent Children's Illustrated Classics, 1949, pages 128-9

122 Wilhelm Humbolt, quoted in Barnstone, page 42

115 Michael Ignatieff, 'Literature honours its unsung heroes', *The Observer*, 24 March 1991, page 21

Justin Kaplan: *Mr Clemens and Mark Twain* (1967), Harmondsworth: Pelican Books, Penguin, 1970

77 Hugh Kingsmill, quoted in Quigly, page 70

124-5, 125 Milan Kundera, *Testaments Betrayed*, translated by Linda Asher, Faber & Faber, 1995, pages 108-9, 110-11

26 Emmanuel Levinas, *Quatre Lectures Talmudiques*, translated by Annette Aronowicz as 'Four Talmudic Readings', Bloomington, Ind., 1990

169 D.F. McKenzie, quoted in Cavallo and Chartier, page 3

43 Adrian Mitchell, *The Listener*, 16 January 1986, page 24

Stanley Morison, *Talbot Baines Reed: Author, Bibliographer, Typefounder* (1960), privately printed at the University Press, Cambridge, 55/*59*, 55-6/*61-2*, 58/*15*, 60/*19*, 61/*19-20*, 72/*10*, 76/*26*, 77/*34*

82-3 Jenny Pausacker, *More than Forty Years On: A historical study of the school story.* Submitted for the degree of Doctor of Pholosophy in the School of Humanities of the Flinders University of South Australia, July 1980, pages 40-3

Penguin Companion to Literature, Harmondsworth: Penguin Books, 1969

Peter Pohl, *Janne, min vän*, Stockholm: AWE/Gebers, 1985

Peter Pohl, *Johnny, my friend*, Woodchester: Turton & Chambers, 1991

Isobel Quigly, *The Heirs of Tom Brown*, London: Chatto & Windus, 1982, 70-1/*53-4*, 77/*43*, *70*. Reprinted by permission of the Random House Group.

57-8 Talbot Baines Reed, quoted in Morison, page 57. Quotations from Reed's novels are taken from the following editions.

Talbot Baines Reed, *The Cock-house at Fellsgarth* (1893), London: Office of 'The Boy's Own Paper', n.d.
Talbot Baines Reed, *The Fifth Form at St Dominic's: A School Story* (1887), with a prefatory note by G.A. Hutchison, London: The Religious Tract Society (The Boy's Own Bookshelf), n.d.
Talbot Baines Reed, *The Master of the Shell* (1894), London: The Religious Tract Society, c.1894
Talbot Baines Reed, *The Willoughby Captains* (1887), London: Latimer House, 1948
Maud Reuterswärd, *Noah Is My Name,* Woodchester: Turton & Chambers, 1991
80 Paul Ricoeur, 'Self as *Ipse*', *Freedom and Interpretation: The Oxford Amnesty Lectures 1992*, edited by Barbara Johnson, New York: Basic Books, 1993, 115
122 A. W. Schlegel, quoted in Barnstone, page 19
126 Schleiermacher, F.E.D., quoted in Stolt, page 131
33, 34 Patricia Meyer Spacks, *The Adolescent Idea: Myths of Youth and the Adult Imagination*, New York: Basic Books, 1981, pages 45, 296
27-8 George Steiner, *No Passion Spent: Essays 1978-1996*, London: Faber & Faber, 1996, page 36
123, 123-4 Birgit Stolt, 'How Emil Becomes Michel', *Children's Books in Translation: The Situation and the Problems*, edited by Göte Klingberg, Mary Ørvig & Stuart Amor, Swedish Institute for Children's Books, Stockholm: Almqvist & Wiskell International, 1978, pages 134-7
51 *A Token for Friends*, being A Memoir of Edgar Osborne, An Appreciation of The Osborne Collection of Early Children's Books and A Facsimile of His Catalogue 'From Morality & Instruction to Beatrix Potter', Toronto: The Friends of the Osborne and Lillian H. Smith Collections, Toronto Public Library, 1979, page 21
Meriol Trevor, *The Arnolds: Thomas Arnold and His Family*, London: Bodley Head, 1973, 63/*23*, 64/*24*, 65-6/*24-7*, 69/*40*. Reprinted by permission of The Random House Group Ltd.
37, 40 Lionel Trilling, *The Liberal Imagination: Essays on Literature and Society* (1951), Harmondsworth: Peregrine Books, Penguin, 1970, pages 114, 117
Mark Twain. See Samuel Clemens. Quotations from Twain's novels are taken from the following editions.
Mark Twain, *The Adventures of Huckleberry Finn* (1884), Harmondsworth: Penguin, 1953
Mark Twain, *The Adventures of Tom Sawyer* (1876), Harmondsworth: Penguin, 1950
36 Mark Twain, quoted in Kaplan, page 275
149 Tarjei Vesaas, *The Ice Palace*, translated by Elizabeth Rokkan, London: Peter Owen, 1966, page 32
120 Lev Vygotsky, *Thought and Language*, newly revised translation by Alex Kozulin, editor, Cambridge MA: MIT Press, 1986, pages 221-2

INDEX